On Un/Certainty

On Un/Certainty

The Uses of Doubt in Dangerous Times

Natasha Lennard

VERSO
London • New York

First published by Verso 2026

The manufacturer's authorized representative in the EU for product safety (GPSR) is LOGOS EUROPE, 9 rue Nicolas Poussin, 17000, La Rochelle, France
contact@logoseurope.eu

1 3 5 7 9 10 8 6 4 2

Verso
UK: 6 Meard Street, London W1F 0EG
US: 207 East 32nd Street, New York, NY 10016
versobooks.com

Verso is the imprint of New Left Books

ISBN-13: 978-1-80429-561-8
ISBN-13: 978-1-80429-565-6 (US EBK)
ISBN-13: 978-1-80429-562-5 (UK EBK)

British Library Cataloguing in Publication Data
A catalogue record for this book is available from the British Library

Library of Congress Cataloging-in-Publication Data
A catalog record for this book is available from the Library of Congress

Typeset in Fournier by Hewer Text UK Ltd, Edinburgh
Printed and bound by CPI Group (UK) Ltd, Croydon, CR0 4YY

Contents

Introduction: On Un/Certainty

Nothing is over, that is the only certainty.
The other certainty is that everything ends, even this.
Joshua Clover, "Poem (September 26, 2023)"

We live in uncertain times. Or so I have been told, again and again. A chorus has emerged. Fundraising politicians, morning news roundups, my university administrators, utilities companies, nonprofits, friends and strangers—they all agree: We live in uncertain times.

"In these uncertain times," the messages begin, and there's little mystery as to why the phrase has been resonating. Amid potent fascist rule, environmental decimation, genocide, world-altering technological shifts, deadly and disabling pandemics—among other crises—there is reason for dread.

Talk of uncertain times hits the right mark for enough people, or so it seems. Uncertain times discourse is so constant that it has become a joke of sorts—"You want to get a drink?" I text a friend. "In these uncertain times?" Think of Brecht, parodied: *In the uncertain times, will there also be posting? Yes, there will also be posting. About the uncertain times.*

The poetry of quotidian speech is full of vague and nonetheless meaningful descriptions that capture moods and provoke responses. So it is with talk of "these uncertain times": It captures that fear abounds, and it registers that we can have no confidence about the nature of our collective futures.

But, then again, in this moment of purported boundless uncertainty, I'm seeing a lot of what looks like certainty in action.

In a video shared by members of the Israeli military on social media in 2024, a soldier walks through the rubble of Al-Azhar University. "To those who say, 'There is no education in Gaza,' " he says, "we bombed them all. Too bad." Within the first one hundred days of the genocide, Israel systematically destroyed every single university on the Gaza strip. These were not uncertain acts.

One group of international medics volunteering in Gaza reported treating 114 Palestinian children who had been shot in the head or chest; single bullets delivered by Israeli snipers—the sort of shots taken with certainty.

Closer to home, masked US Immigration and Customs Enforcement agents move through courthouses, factories, and residential neighborhoods with steely purpose. They drag cab drivers from cars, chase farmworkers across fields, and pull weeping mothers from their wailing children; they surrounded an international student on a quiet Massachusetts street as she walked to meet friends to break her Ramadan fast. She screamed as masked men surrounded her, one grabbed her wrists. Passersby thought Rümeysa Öztürk was being kidnapped—and she was. By the federal government, which aimed to deport her over an op-ed she cowrote in her university newspaper, calling on the school to divest from Israel's war machine. Öztürk had no idea why she was being detained, but her uncertainty was not the problem. The agents moved with certainty.

The countless gleeful posts online—"I voted for this!" under videos of shackled brown men—those posts sound pretty certain, too. The repeated demand by anti-trans crusaders that we "define woman!" when, for them, only an exclusionary definition will do—they are also quite certain.

In each of these cases, the operations of certainty, rather than uncertainty, give me the greatest cause for concern. Yet we hear all too rarely of certainty *in these uncertain times*. This is a problem.

Only the foolhardy might recommend more uncertainty in these circumstances. I am also not suggesting, with these opening examples, that acting with certainty is the sole preserve of authoritarian leaders and jackbooted thugs. My point is this: We must pay more attention to what gets to be held certain today, and what does not. We must also ask what role all our talk of uncertainty plays.

I started to note pervasive doubt as if it were a purposeful mood some time in 2020. Historian Beans Velocci has also highlighted that, during the height of the Covid-19 pandemic, a barrage of "uncertain times" messaging spoke to a strategic manufacturing of "not-knowing." This, they argued, enabled powerful actors to evade responsibility with extreme discriminatory effects. It is convenient to gesture wildly, and often invalidly, toward uncertainty to keep hierarchies and hegemonies firmly in place, producing violence of which we can be certain.

This is the driving animus of this book. It is not an argument for or against uncertainty, or for or against certainty. Rather, it is a call for better certainties. And in order for that to make sense, we must draw our attention to specific *activities* of certainty and doubt that shape the terrains of our current struggles. I want to track pernicious certainty in action and see how it infiltrates the operations of white supremacy, ethnonationalism, the presumption of border regimes, property logics, trans-exclusionary ideology, and other oppressive world-ordering commitments.

Why? Because we must look at the work of certainty in these terrains in order to build a timely counterhegemonic force. For I see an urgent need to reroute our uncertainty discourse; I see liberatory potential in doing so. We must address what gets held all too certain by all too many, and what that certainty entails, if we are to forge a world of better certainties, as I believe we must.

For this task, I turn to an unlikely theoretical guide for contemporary leftists: Austrian-British twentieth-century philosopher Ludwig Wittgenstein.

QUESTIONS OF DOUBT, certainty, and knowledge have long occupied philosophers. Few, I believe, have taken up the issue in as compelling a manner as Wittgenstein. Published in 1969, eighteen years after the philosopher's death, *On Certainty* is a collection of notes written in the final years of Wittgenstein's life that offer an invaluable roadmap through which we can begin to appreciate how uncertainty and certainty work. The notes are, by turns, exercises in analytic argumentation, lapidary aphorism, open questioning, and therapeutic monologue.

Wittgenstein hacks away at the centuries-old problem of Cartesian doubt: How do we answer radical skeptics who believe that it is impossible to truly know anything at all? Is not everything open to doubt? Rather than leading us to a stabilizing cogito, as Descartes did, Wittgenstein—in line with his late philosophical approach—exposes the workings of certainty and doubt by drawing attention to language games in which the activities of being certain or having doubt are necessarily embedded. Typical philosophical puzzles, Wittgenstein points out, miss something crucial about the operations of certainty and uncertainty, as well as what it is to know or not-know something. We cannot doubt everything, he posits, but that does not mean we *know* all those things we cannot doubt.

Our talk today of "uncertain times" conjures a scene of unending, boundless doubt in need of an intervention like Wittgenstein's. Like the radical skeptic, we too often fail to attend to the actual workings of doubt, knowledge, and certainty.

We frame the uncertainty of our times as totalizing, but Wittgenstein points out that uncertainty—the activity of doubting—has a necessary stopping point. As he wrote: "If you tried to doubt everything you would not get as far as doubting anything. The game of doubting itself presupposes certainty."

Wittgenstein here is characteristically gnomic, but in one sense the claim is about ordinary language. In our normal usage, "doubt" is not applied to, say, the existence of physical objects. In almost any instance, if someone were to attempt to really doubt everything—from the existence of physical objects to the fact that the world has existed since long before our births—we would simply conclude that they were mentally disturbed, or high. "If you are not certain of any fact," Wittgenstein notes, "you cannot be certain of the meaning of your words either." Without some structuring certainties, doubt cannot get off the ground.

You cannot, for example, ask meaningful questions about specific objects in the world—"Is there any wine left in the bottle?"—without holding certain at the time of questioning that physical objects exist. You cannot meaningfully ask a specific question about an historic event—"When was the Russian Revolution?"—if, at the same time, you also doubt whether the earth existed before your birth. Even the radical skeptic, therefore, holds certain things, well, certain, in order to engage in a game of doubting in the first place.

Each act of uncertainty or doubting requires what Wittgenstein calls (somewhat elusively) a "hinge"—an epistemic ballast held certain and unquestionable. "The questions that we raise and our doubts depend on the fact that some propositions are exempt from doubt, are as it were like hinges on which those turn," he notes. "If I want the door to turn, the hinges must stay put." Whatever uncertainties we may have today, however existential they may feel, Wittgenstein reminds us that they stop somewhere.

Wittgenstein uses another key image to express this: the riverbed. All our doubting and knowing needs to flow through the certain "riverbed of thoughts," the "bedrock" of our believing. The riverbed represents what cannot be doubted at a given time and place; it determines the speed, flow and direction of ideas and frameworks of understanding. But as we will see, the flowing river also has an eroding effect that can, over time, create meanders, new streams and tributaries and dams.

So, the riverbed, in this metaphor, is what we cannot doubt at a given time. But what are we left with at the end of doubt? It's tempting to say "knowledge." And we do indeed treat our uncertainties with acts of knowledge gathering, checking, learning and proving. Wittgenstein points out that our activities of knowing and doubting necessarily work together: If I say that I know something, I can be asked, "How do you know it?" and I can give further grounds and justifications for my purported knowledge.

If I say, for example, "I know there is a genocide in Gaza," and am met with doubt, I can offer a wealth of further proof that grounds my knowledge claim. When we make knowledge claims about a whole host of political commitments, we can marshal swathes of evidence: If I say, for another example, "I know that trans kids need gender-affirming care," I can back that up. But we all know what it's like to hit a brick wall in political arguments, when we have met every question of doubt with more proof of knowledge, but no amount of evidence or information will persuade our opponent, and we run out of justifications to offer.

Knowledge, to return to our metaphor, is not the hard riverbed where doubting stops—it is part of the river's flow. Because, as Wittgenstein illuminates, at the end of our doubting we do not find knowledge but certainty—a more unwieldy beast.

IT IS COMMON to think that certainty is simply a type of knowledge—a settled knowledge, possessed of the highest level of justification. Not so, argues Wittgenstein, pointing to the notable difference between the activities of knowing and those of being certain.

We can offer further evidence or justification for the things we know: I know, for example, that the 5 train runs from President Street, or that the Industrial Revolution relied upon the bloody fruits of slavery, or that vaccines save millions of lives. What we know, we can also technically doubt—we can ask, "How do I know this?" and gather evidence to counter that doubt and so justify our knowledge claims. Certainty works differently; certainties are, according to Wittgenstein, those propositions held exempt from doubt, the very hinges on which our questioning about the world turns.

Again, as Wittgenstein notes, our certainties are the "bedrock" of our believing—no further grounds or justifications can be offered for a certainty that are *more convincing than the certainty itself*. Let's use Wittgenstein's key example, taken from his fellow philosopher G. E. Moore: that I'm certain that I have two hands. And I really am certain that I have two hands. But there's no *deeper justification* I can give you for this conviction than just . . . showing you my two hands. This is not an activity of knowing—I do not develop knowledge in terms of a justified true belief about the existence of my hands—but I am indeed certain of their existence; I act with this certainty all day, every day when using my hands.

Many certainties are banal like this classic example: We are certain that physical objects, like our hands, exist. We hold commitments like this certain, but we also cannot offer more compelling grounds or point to deeper justifications for them. They are immune from doubt but unlike other posits of knowledge, they are not proven with further evidence or proofs. We do not learn to know these certainties like we might learn to know an empirical fact or a mathematical formula. Yet we are indeed certain of them. Wittgenstein thus highlights that certainties function as a special class of convictions that are not claims to knowledge but that are nevertheless foundational within our collective practices. At any given time, our certainties form the riverbed of our language game, which, Wittgenstein notes, "is not based on grounds. It is not reasonable (or unreasonable). It is there—like our life."

Not all certainties are banal; not all are universally shared. Wittgenstein wrote his final reflections, for example, two decades before the moon landing, and as he noted, it was held certain that walking on the moon was impossible: "If we are thinking within our system, then it is certain that no one has ever been on the moon," he wrote. In his example, he imagines meeting a man who nonetheless claims vehemently to have recently traveled to the moon. "We should feel ourselves intellectually very distant from someone who said this," the philosopher noted. He could be *certain* that the man had not been to the moon; not because he checked and tested the man's knowledge and background and deemed that his story happened to be false, but because getting to the moon was understood to be impossible, as a point of certainty.

It's a telling example—a bedrock certainty that has since shifted. Wittgenstein's moon example also shows that what he's talking about in terms of certainties is not limited only to truisms like "external objects exist." Instead, his framework applies to a whole array of collective commitments that are deemed beyond doubt, but not because we have checked and verified their correctness. The point of the example is to show that a person who appears to doubt what is certain is dismissed not simply as incorrect in one specific judgment, but in their ability to share in our judgments at all.

Wittgenstein's concept of certainty, then, applies to all such world-ordering convictions, which—for those who share them—it literally makes no sense to doubt. And, as we'll see, that includes the tenets of dominant ideology—my interest in this book.

As I say, most of the certainties of daily life are unremarkable—we don't doubt them and that's not a problem. But many violent certainties abound, too—harmful commitments held fast, which discipline the very shape of how and what it is considered reasonable to doubt. The terrain of what gets held certain is not neutral. Meaning making is necessarily collective, but that does not make it democratic, or just. Too often we see the brutal consequences of this.

We might consider, for example, the many shared language games and background forms of life in which white supremacy is held by some to be no less certain than the existence of their hands. I'm not proposing that white supremacist or ethnonationalist beliefs are certainties for some people in the exact same universal way as a constant certainty about the existence of external objects, but they do function as world-ordering certainties. It speaks to a morbid terrain of certainty that cops and civilian vigilantes can kill Black children in the name of self-defense and have confidence that a court will agree; the undergirding certainty, which is lived out without needing to be stated, is that of white standing. These are violent certainties, but they still work like certainties: shared practices that serve as the stopping point for doubt, the hinges on which other propositions about the world get to turn.

IN THE CHAPTERS that follow, I address the work of certainty and the weaponization of doubt across some of the key terrains of contemporary struggle. The topics I address—the concept of crisis today; border rule; anti-trans pronatalism; the limits of evidence and witnessing in antiracist, anticolonial struggles—are all areas in which uncertainty is misused and abused, and pernicious certainties go unrecognized for the riverbeds that they are.

This is not, of course, a full survey of the workings of uncertainty today. Each chapter, rather, is an interrogation of a specific, and harmful certainty, and the ways it is held fast through a constellation of activities and practices. For the most part, things held certain—like border rule, or property relations—are not taught explicitly. Instead, they are transmitted as practices, background assumptions, or hinges that organize how a system's beneficiaries, and even its victims, might see the world. For those for whom white supremacy is a certainty, for example, empirical truths that challenge its standing as a hinge are a priori rejected.

We know, for example, that nation-states do not transcend history, but we are also taught, implicitly but constantly, that we must act within and under border regimes. Those of us who would challenge this ordering regime and highlight its contingency are seen as unhinged from the realm of realpolitik. Like the radical skeptics whose doubts only make sense in a specialized philosophical context, anti-border activists are dismissed as entertaining that which cannot be entertained. In the same way, while talk of "uncertain times" characterized the pandemic's early years, the certainties of capital—make work and let die—continued to prove world-ordering in ways far beyond the uncertain behaviors of the novel coronavirus. The terrains of certainty and uncertainty I examine are all unavoidably shaped by the operations of capitalism: the profit motive, private ownership, the drive to growth. My aim is not to simply restate Fredric Jameson's point, popularized by theorist Mark Fisher, that "it is easier to imagine the end of the world than the end of capitalism." Rather, I want to interrogate various practices of doubting, knowing, and being certain that help hold these horizons of imagination in place.

It might sound like I'm using "certainty" here as a synonym for "ideology." All ideology is indeed undergirded by certainty in the way Wittgenstein frames it, but not all certainties function as ideology. Certainty about the existence of external objects is not ideological. But why then, when it comes to political struggle, talk about certainty at all, and not just use concepts like ideology, or hegemony, or other terms more common to left-wing theorizing?

For me, Wittgenstein's understanding of certainty conveys something harder to budge, once it is held stable as a collective episteme. With similarities to, but key epistemological differences from, Antonio Gramsci's conception of common sense, Wittgenstein's certainty framework offers a way to understand dominant ideologies, and, crucially, to appreciate why it's so hard to shift entrenched ideological commitments; we must change the conditions under which they're held certain. As such, deploying Wittgenstein's concept of certainty speaks to the need for collective shifts toward more liberatory forms of life, an unsettling of fascist bedrock.

Wittgenstein did not deploy his work on this subject—nor any other—to explicitly political purposes. But I'm hardly the first to find his reflections richly applicable to the ends of political thought and discursive interventions. Scholars like Alice Crary, Rupert

Read, and Cressida Heyes, among others, approach questions of Wittgenstein's ethical and political uses with inspiring rigor. With my explorations here, I use Wittgenstein's reflections for my own purposes and do not claim to be offering a correct or novel interpretation of his work. Rather, I take up Read's invitation to see a liberatory philosophy in Wittgenstein—to follow Wittgenstein's reminder that "the sickness of a time is cured by an alteration in the mode of life of human beings, and it is possible for the sickness of philosophical problems to get cured only through a changed mode of thought and of life, not through a medicine invented by an individual."

Like his work on language and meaning more broadly, Wittgenstein's *On Certainty* addresses certainty, doubt and knowledge not as abstracted and tightly predefined concepts, but rather as lived activities that come into being through shared use—everyday life, in other words. And it is in this spirit that I suggest we refocus our thoughts on uncertainty and its limits. For such reflections to be put to liberatory use, though, it will be necessary to pair them with the crucial interventions of abolitionist, Black radical, feminist, anticapitalist thinkers, as I do throughout this text.

WITTGENSTEIN'S description of certainties as forming the riverbed of our thoughts is telling. Riverbeds, after all, are subject to shifting. We "distinguish between the movement of the waters on the river-bed and the shift of the bed itself; though there is not a sharp division of the one from the other." As he also notes, "Men have believed that they could make the rain." What was once certain permits of doubt in a different circumstance. "What men and women consider reasonable alters," writes Wittgenstein. "At certain periods, men and women find reasonable what at other periods they found unreasonable. And vice versa." This is not, crucially, some affirmation of liberal progress narratives: that we tend toward greater knowledge and banish poorer thinking. Rather, it's to note that certainties—on which doubting depends—are always situated in material, historical conditions.

Nonetheless, at a single, given moment, a riverbed functions as a stable object. Likewise, philosopher Olúfẹ́mi O. Táíwò, in his call for constructive climate-focused reparations, describes how "the stones of the aqueducts that contain and discipline the continuous motion of the past into the future were laid in the seventeenth, eighteenth, and nineteenth centuries." He notes, "The patterns in how advantage and disadvantage flow have changed very little . . . We can tell, because things still fundamentally move in the same directions." The world order of "global racial empire," as Táíwò helpfully describes it, has not been undone. The container of the motion of history and its violences can appear immovable.

In the face of world-ordering certainties, we must reckon with a key challenge: It rarely works to convince someone out of a given certainty through debate, through reason, or even with the presentation of evidence—if something is held to be foundational, challenges to it are dismissed or explained away, rather than incorporated into the person's worldview. The world often has to change sufficiently, such that previously held certainties can no longer operate as such—consider, again, Wittgenstein's moon example.

"The difficulty is to realize the groundlessness of our believing," Wittgenstein notes. But that does not condemn us to thinking all certainties have equal worth and must be left to stand or fall in the winds of time, even while we might not be able to offer some deeper proof for their being true while we hold them. Philosopher

Amia Srinivasan has written about how "critical genealogists" have been made anxious about the fact that their beliefs and representations about the world have specific, historically contingent origins; born in a different time, place, context, they'd likely have different ones. But that doesn't mean our believing is some sort of moral free-for-all. "The crucial question for such critical genealogists," notes Srinivasan, is not are "our representations true, but what do our representations do? What practices and forms of life do they help sustain, what sort of person do they help construct, and whose power do they help entrench?" We can apply the same approach to our discussion of certainty, particularly since, for Wittgenstein, our certainties are always manifested or expressed in our ways of acting. We act with the certainty that external objects exist; we don't attempt to walk through walls.

Certainties are not, after all, simply representations of the world, but ways of ordering the world as we live in it. And we can observe the consequences of widely held certainties. On the everyday level, we see that it is necessary to hold several things certain; our certainty in the existence of external objects, for example, is necessary for us to talk meaningfully about any object in particular. But we uphold that certainty not by repeating it or relearning it or by stating its truth, but by living with it as certain. We pass each other wine and food, we hold each other, we open doors, we carry groceries, we march down streets—together.

When it comes to acting with political and ethical certainty, we can demonstrate, in the world, that antifascist, anticapitalist, antiracist, abolitionist, feminist, and trans-celebratory commitments produce conditions of possibility for less suffering and greater flourishing. And it is through our actions that those commitments can be shored up as certainties. I do not need to—in fact I likely cannot—convince a committed anti-trans interlocutor that trans women are women. And trans people should not need to prove it to anyone else, ever. It's a certainty, one among many world-ordering hinges, which we help ensure as an unchallenged, lived reality by acting collectively, en masse—supporting our trans comrades, celebrating trans kids.

Equally, it's not uncertain what the consequences are of holding fast to oppressive certainties: to border regimes, white supremacy, sex and gender binaries, and capitalist labor and property relations; such certainties ensure mass death and immiseration. We can rarely convince fascists of the falsity of what they hold fast, but we can take antifascist action to make upholding these certainties intolerable enough that it becomes preferable to abandon them. We can and must collectively act outside and against such fascist certainties, such that their uncertainty—and in turn their falsehood—is made plain.

Act, that is, with the certainties on which we want our practices to hinge; only then can we begin to dream of more joyful uncertainties.

1
Certain Crises

It is the air of atrocity,
An event as ordinary
As a President.

A plume of smoke, visible at a distance
In which people burn.

George Oppen, *On Being Numerous*

I'VE BEEN THINKING about crisis.

We take for granted that "crisis" is the correct way to describe everything from the Great Recession of 2008–2009 to the deadly contamination of the water in Flint, Michigan, to accelerating climate decimation to the collapse of popular faith in liberal institutions to a global pandemic to mounting tensions between nuclear powers, and so much more. In recent years "polycrisis," a term coined in the 1990s by sociologist Edgar Morin and more recently popularized by economic historian Adam Tooze, has caught on in international policy circles and beyond with little resistance. Crises, overlapping, entangled, mutually escalating—sounds about right.

But how can it be that crisis—typically understood as a rupture, when the contradictions of what was once settled are condensed and exposed—is itself the settled thing? When crisis is a permanent state, taken almost as a given of common sense, can we even speak meaningfully of crisis? Debates continue around the applicability of various Marxist theories of capitalist crises to our current economic realities, in which the question persists: capitalism—how does it end? Does it end? With the idea in mind that any contemporary crisis is a complex constellation, irreducible to but inseparable from conditions of capitalist production, I want to reflect instead on the ubiquitousness of crisis talk. "Why should crisis, as a category, be so self-evident?" asks anthropologist Janet Roitman.

We do speak of crises all the time, and we make sense while doing so—we don't fail to communicate with the word. If I ask, for example, "Is there a border crisis?" you surely understand what I mean; how you answer, though, will likely tell me more about how you relate to border regimes than how you necessarily interpret the term "crisis." As Tooze has put it, "Show me your crisis and I will tell you who you are."

Although often used as just another synonym for "catastrophe" or "disaster," "crisis" remains conceptually distinct. In some ways the categorization is uncomplicated enough: If something is delineated as a crisis, rather than, say, just a disaster or a tragedy, the implication is that we're talking about a situation in which there appears, however faintly, a possibility of resolution. Crises are unresolved; that is, a crisis—what gets called a crisis in the present—definitionally demands resolution but currently lacks one.

Etymology is no accurate guide to contemporary use, but I'm interested in the fact that these terms originate in the activities of judgment and valuation, rather than ideas of value-free knowledge formation about a given state of affairs. "Crisis" and "certain" are cognates: the morpheme, *krei-*, "to sieve, to distinguish, to discriminate," is the root of both the Latin *cernere*, "to distinguish, decide" (the origin of "certain"), and the Greek *krisis*, "turning point, judgment, result of a trial." It performs, with differing levels of conviction and desperation, a call to action.

However, "crisis" in modern usage remains conceptually tied to acts of decision not yet made. As such, uncertainty is the bedfellow of crisis: decisions need making, actions need to be taken, and there is doubt as to what is to be done. But when the "what" is known, doubt then circles around how it is to be done. Take the need for mass and swift atmospheric decarbonization: the *what* is no mystery, the challenge of *how* keeps the crisis unresolved with terrifying consequences. Unsurprisingly, then, talk of crisis and talk of uncertainty are bound together.

Current norms of crisis response are like an unending game of planet-sized Whack-A-Mole, until we can't see the ground for the mole holes, until it's all churned-up dirt from which nothing new can grow. But in this metaphor, to be clear, the ruling classes by definition hold the mallet. This is the game of crisis management today.

But if broad talk of uncertain times distracts our attention from numerous harmful certainties, then constant talk of an age of crisis can perform its own bewitching. Roitman has argued that crisis functions as a "blind spot . . . which makes certain things visible and others invisible":

> Crisis is never itself explained because it is necessarily further reduced to other elements, such as capitalism, economy, neoliberalism, finance, politics, culture, subjectivity. In that sense, crisis is not a condition to be observed . . . it is an observation that produces meaning. More precisely, it is a distinction that secures "a world" for observation.

Crisis is always a second-order concept; it is not an object of direct observation but an analytic frame that allows us to observe—in particular to frame situations, when things appear to fall apart. In this way, crisis narratives can be said to organize time, in which geographies, temporalities, agents, and actions take on the weight of historical meaning. We speak of crisis and reach back to locate beginnings, causes, progressions.

Take the 2008 subprime mortgage crisis. Here Roitman interrogates the conditions needed for the series of events to be deemed a crisis:

> At what point do houses figured as equity become figured as debt? At what point do subprime mortgage bonds transform from an asset to a liability? And the ultimate question: When does the judgment of crisis obtain?

Roitman's point is that thinking the world in terms of crisis "regulates narrative constructions" of history, of social and political order, in certain ways; "it allows certain questions to be asked while others are foreclosed . . . The point is to take note of the effects of the claim to crisis, to be attentive to the effects of our very accession to that judgment."

THE CURRENT talk of crisis is haunted—the ghosts of centuries of meaning making echo through our motley usage. German theorist of history Reinhart Koselleck first noted over half a century ago that "crisis" had become a "slogan (*Schlagwort*)": "Because of its metaphorical flexibility . . . it enters into everyday language."

Koselleck maps out a hauntology of sorts, revealing the past usages that attend our contemporary meanings of "crisis." Digging through the sedimentation of conceptual history, Koselleck shows how "crisis" brings with it layers of theological, medical, and juridical associations. The origin of "crisis" in the classical Greek meaning "decision" or "judgment" applied in the legal, constitutional sense, and in the theological sense of "the last judgment." Without its theological origin, Koselleck notes, crisis qua final judgment "is a question of recasting a theological principle of belief. It is expected of world-immanent history itself."

We are the first generation(s) for whom an increasingly uninhabitable planet is a coming and widely observed reality. The history of the concept of crisis should, however, remind us that we are not the first with an orientation to end times. As philosopher Geoff Mann has noted:

> This is not the first time the world has seemed to teeter on a precipice. The philosopher Hannah Arendt, writing in the shadow of Cold War nuclear buildup more than half a century ago, assessed her own time in a phrase that resonates today: "to the question how shall we ever be able to extricate ourselves from the obvious insanity of this position, there is no answer." Then, as now, we knew very little about how the menacing future might unfold, and how much time we might have had to avert it, if that were possible. Then, as now, apocalyptic thinking was not confined to Chicken Littles or street-corner preachers; indeed, it had become, paradoxically, quite normal.

European expansion was notably apocalyptic for entire Indigenous worlds and knowledge systems. Entire forms of life have been eradicated before. Yet today's apocalypticism may come with the specific shock of a broken promise: that modernity and growth, history's supposed end, did not deliver an end to end times. It's nonetheless a privileged relation to end times to imagine them *only* as a future threat. Tell that to the people of Gaza. As Mann also points out, our knowledge of the facts of climate change does not inform the ways we act in accordance with the weight of that knowledge:

> What is uncertain is not conflict, heat, and volatility, but how we will adapt to it, who we will become. But this does little if anything to diminish the vastness of the inescapable horizon . . . Even if "human extinction" were where we are headed, we are hardly less at a loss. The only thing we know is how it ends. Between here and there—almost nothing.

Narratives of eschatological crisis and overwhelming uncertainty pervade as if we did not already have the relevant understanding and tools to radically curb climate decimation. Yet in the face of this knowledge, capitalism continues in its certain logic, a will to profit foreclosing the changes we already know are necessary.

Nowhere is this more extreme, or more deranging, than in discourses around the future of artificial intelligence technologies. Here, a classical variety of crisis narrative pervades, with thick theological valence: a threshold is supposedly approaching, which could lead to the destruction of life on earth, or our salvation.

We are told that the magic of AI—and it is described with no more concreteness than a few gestures to conjuring—could solve every worldly problem and more, from climate devastation to poverty to illness to (for those who see our mortal coil as a problem to solve) mortality itself. All it requires is the sacrifice of trillions of dollars, untold swaths of land, energy from fossil fuels, and invisibilized human labor. Consider how tech multibillionaires Bill Gates and Eric Schmidt have brushed off the issue of AI processing's already ruinous, gargantuan consumption of energy and water use.

AI, Schmidt told the *New York Times*, "had too much potential, to let concerns about climate change get in the way."

As cognitive scientist Hagen Blix and machine learning researcher Ingeborg Glimmer noted in their 2025 critique of popular AI narratives, *Why We Fear AI*: "We don't need 'superintelligence' to know what's causing climate change—we already know. We are failing to stop climate change because capitalism stands in the way, not because we lack intelligence. Ultimately, intelligence isn't the problem, so superintelligence isn't the solution."

Instead of a serious reckoning with actually existing harms and possibilities of technological development, technocapital's mouthpieces prefer a story of an inevitable judgment day: the great thinking machines are coming and will destroy or deliver us. Pesky questions about the actual capacities and potentials of machine learning are brushed aside. So, too, are difficult discussions about the dark history of intelligence as a calculable quality and a messy, contested concept. Genuine uncertainties and unknowns about how best (or not) to develop and deploy advanced machine learning technologies are obviated—such considerations being reserved for the Great Men of Silicon Valley. Uncertainty and doubt about the control and distribution of earthly resources are replaced with a myth of our inevitable replacement, for existentially better or worse.

The grand crisis narratives get stranger still. Philosopher Alice Crary has highlighted how an entire cottage industry of philosophers and researchers has been generously funded by Silicon Valley interests for well over a decade to help frame the supposedly moral debate around AI's uncertain future as one of "existential risk," using grim consequentialist logic and abstract calculations that lead to repugnant conclusions. According to this so-called longtermist philosophy, humans are merely vessels of potential, bearers of some sort of calculable measure of well-being or "value." An "x-risk" refers not to the pedestrian ravages of war, disease, and climate destruction as we might think of them in a lived sense. It is, rather, a eugenicist fairytale in which elite humans create elite superhuman intelligences that will proliferate in the trillions for trillions of years, creating the greatest sum of value. The risk applies not to our collective flourishing, but to the failure to reach this "potential." As Crary noted in a recent lecture, this risk framework "echoes the reasoning of fascist dictators and sci-fi villains (e.g., Thanos in the Marvel Universe) who aren't averse to mass death if it brings on futures they hail as utopia." Or these superintelligences could destroy everything before such a bountiful future is realized. Either way, some messianic crisis point is posited such that, even if it's only a miniscule future possibility, expected value calculations demand that unprecedented resources be sacrificed to it.

Keynes once warned against treating genuine future uncertainty as reducible to calculable risk; such guidance has, of course, been long abandoned to decades of speculative market logic invading every field. Professional philosophers today are given significant book deals and millions in institutional funding to do fantastical calculations about the probability of a superintelligence-filled galaxy billions of years hence, or the total annihilation of life on earth in nearer centuries. This is what passes in mainstream analytic philosophy today for questions about moral uncertainty.

I'm hardly the first to note that those who warn of AI dystopia or rave about AI utopia call for the same sort of crisis management—stratospheric investment in AI and related research is required either way. And it is precisely the beneficiaries of the AI gold rush—the venture capitalists, founders, CEOs, and favored so-called thought leaders—who most fervently push narratives about a great and/or terrible super-AI, and its inevitability. It is convenient to place immediate catastrophes of capitalism in a narrative of a deferred, judgment-day crisis. As Blix and Glimmer note:

> If the stakes are as high as the very survival of humanity, then concerns about the effects that really existing artificial intelligence technology has right now—from excessive energy usage, to undermining the livelihood of artists and dock workers, to introducing cybersecurity vulnerabilities, to perpetuating and worsening discrimination, to disinformation and deep fakes, to supercharging mass surveillance, etc., are easily brushed aside.

"Crisis" has never been reserved for talk of end times alone. Greeks also used it as a medical term for the turning point in a disease, the point at which a patient would either return to health or expire. Contemporary use remains suffused with medical metaphor: economies are in crisis or healthy. Economists and journalists write of "anemic recoveries," "market ills," and so on. The overheating earth is sick, and at a critical point that could lead to planetary death or restoration to (a sort) of health.

However, for historian Istvan Hont, writing in the mid-'90s era of market globalization, understanding crisis through medical metaphor has been the most misleading analytic of all. A return to health is not an option; nor, for so many things deemed in crisis, is a total death really in the cards. The question is, rather, who gets to live on, and how. Hont suggests that it "might be intellectually productive" to speak not of "crisis" but of "normality":

> What is needed is to get away from the medical metaphor as much as possible. For want of a better option one might suggest that a non-teleological process of permanent "crisis," a sort of process which might lead to survival (or perhaps moderate improvement), but not to full "health," may best be described as historical normality. "Normality," if used skeptically and cautiously, would simply re-define most "crises" as difficulties attendant on "change" . . . If one accepts that "change," however difficult and "crisis-like" its actual experience might be, is "normal," then what is most often called "crisis" is the normal manifestation of political and economic movement, without ever necessarily reaching a grand "crisis" with a conclusively positive or irrevocably negative outcome.

Is Hont correct? Do these nonstop invocations of crisis as something deadly or wholly curable lead us to miss what is just a painful, noncritical normal?

Contrary to the historian, but in line with his concerns, I might submit that a medical metaphor is something worth holding onto; it offers a wholly appropriate sense of crisis if we think of chronic rather than acute illness. Indeed, over half a decade into the mass death event of the Covid pandemic, we know that many illnesses are not simply either terminal or cured, as the ancient notion of medical "crisis" would have it. Illness can be chronic and debilitating, and only ever managed. Consider the insistence on the part of political leaders that, in order to return the economy to "health," the Covid crisis had to be deemed over even as the pandemic still raged on—for the small sacrifice of millions of lives and of the future well-being of millions more.

Whereas Hont writes of abandoning crisis talk in favor of "historical normality," the late cultural theorist Lauren Berlant wrote of a "regime of crisis ordinariness." The idea of "crisis ordinary" demarcates the present in a temporality of perpetual crisis but also attends to the activities of surviving, going on, and wearing out required of those populations designated expendable. "Long-term problems of embodiment within capitalism, in the zoning of the everyday and the work of getting through it," Berlant noted, "are less successfully addressed in the temporalities of crisis and require other frames for understanding the contexts of doing, being, and thriving."

Berlant's suggestion appeals to me. Hont's proposal—that in place of crisis talk, we treat difficult change as a "historical normality" without telos—is clarifying, but it misses something about the textures in the language games of crisis. After all, is there not something going on there, in our constant reliance on this chaotic concept, that we don't simply abandon it to talk instead of normality and change? We could put this down to poor habits of speech and fuzzy meaning making. But I venture that would foreclose the psychic stakes of the crisis narratives on which we do rely.

Because there remains, at least notionally, something hopeful in the constant talk of crisis: a refusal to accept these dismal circumstances as a normality to be no more than managed. "Crisis" does still conjure, to at least some extent, the promise or threat of rupture, the hint of revolutionary possibility. "From the seventeenth century on, the term, used as a metaphor, expanded into politics, economics, history, psychology," writes Koselleck. "Towards the end of the eighteenth century, the term once again took on religious and theological connotations; but by its application to the events of the French and American revolutions, the apocalyptic vision of the last judgment now required secular meaning."

This modern sense of the word, which Koselleck finds first in Rousseau, permits a notion of crisis that is at once a cyclical event, a set of causes, a transitional phase, a culmination, and an inevitability. The term is promiscuous in its reflexivity, jumping imperceptibly between describing a state of affairs and the experience of experiencing a state of affairs: "Once 'crisis' had become a commonly employed expression, its use became an indicator of both the intensity of a crisis and the perception of it as such." Crucially, though, beginning in the late Enlightenment, as Hont notes, with reference to Koselleck, "crisis became twinned with the idea of revolution."

Since the act of designating something a crisis is one that, per Roitman, produces meaning, it's perhaps less important to ask whether it is true or false that a situation constitutes a "real crisis," with revolutionary potential at hand. The question, rather, is whether and how we can collectively produce such a meaning of crises (or what we keep describing as crises). If not, then, sure, we should probably talk not so much of crisis but of disastrous normality. And I think there would be a loss in that.

YOU'LL NOTE THAT many of the above paragraphs are conspicuously lacking in human agency. Who calls the situation a crisis? Critical decisions need making—by someone? It should be established as a journalistic standard: don't talk of crisis without finishing your sentences—a crisis for whom, a crisis of what, a crisis from what?

Hont noted three decades ago that "it is a characteristic feature of the corruption of modern political language that the notion of 'crisis' is overused, generalized and trivialized." (Of Hont, we might also ask, Corrupted by whom? Trivialized by whom? By what forces and practices?) My goal, however, is not to clean up our political language—there's no sharp line delineating correct and incorrect use of the label "crisis." Like Roitman I want to ask, "What narratives are precluded by the crisis narrative," and which are entrenched? That is to say: I wish to illuminate the way current crisis talk can counterintuitively foreclose rather than open more liberatory horizons. In part, it can do so by failing to distinguish between problems of knowledge and activities of certainty.

I'm far from the first to point out that talk of crisis without agency—without subjects and objects, perpetrators and victims—permits all too much obfuscation of the operations of power and political manipulation. As Israel carried out its genocide, establishment news outlets, along with the wholly complicit White House, described the situation of tens of thousands of Palestinians slaughtered, millions displaced and starved, and the obliteration of all Gaza's major infrastructure as a "humanitarian crisis"—which is both accurate and a darkly convenient phrase by which to accord impunity to Israel as it carried out a project of annihilation, long in the making.

The invocation of crisis permits such equivocal rhetoric because the language game of crisis is riddled with ambiguity and paradox. As noted, a crisis can at once be a state of affairs, its causes, its effects, an end point, a historiographical demarcation, an expression of moral judgment, and an aporia. Does the designation "crisis" really function to compel critique? (Crisis and critique are also cognates, after all.) It can function that way, but often the crisis label, circulated through the news cycle, evacuates the possibility for moral and political judgment. What would we be forced to say, if we couldn't just say "crisis" to describe a scenario? Then we would have to talk of agents and actions, decisions, relations of power, consequences and material conditions.

The historian Tooze was clear on this point when writing on Israel's policy of ethnic cleansing in Gaza by means of starvation.

Referencing other sites of acute hunger around the world in 2025, Tooze wrote in his newsletter, “Sudan, South Sudan, Myanmar, DRC are all in civil war. In Haiti there is anarchy. All these situations might be reasonably described either as zones of polycrisis, or as regions of chronic poverty (Northern Nigeria, for instance)—which itself demands a deeper explanation.” By contrast, he noted, the reasons for famine in Gaza

> are not manifestations of a crisis. They are being conducted with full deliberation by Israel, a rich and fully sovereign state . . . Death by starvation in Gaza is not the collateral, unintended consequence of an obscure, anonymous, amorphous crisis. It is the result of deliberate policy on the part of the Israeli government, bent on using the resources of a highly sophisticated state to render Palestinian life in Gaza impossible.

According to Tooze, for whom polycrisis had been a key analytic, the term “crisis” used by US and other Western politicians to describe Israel’s starvation of Gaza is a “grotesque euphemism.”

Gaza is not the only site for which the term “crisis” is perniciously misleading, but Israel’s genocide makes the violence of this conceptual distortion brutally clear. And this is hardly the first time that Palestine has exposed the intolerable failings of the stories told by the so-called rules-based international order.

THINGS CAN JUST get worse. This should serve as a clear rebuke to any advocates for vulgar accelerationism, who argue for a teleological commitment to hastening and deepening states of crisis to, they say, inevitably bring about revolutionary social change for the better. The problem is hardly that we don’t have enough crises, or crisis enough. If anything, it's extraordinary that we still understand "crisis" as a concept imbued with revolutionary meaning at all; what would it mean to see the potential for rupture in a crisis?

Let the language game of crisis not lead us astray: a grammar of crisis that narrativizes history into points of conjunctural rupture risks failing to recognize the long process that revolutionary shifts require. And that are, as Stuart Hall reminds us, never guaranteed. "Permanent crisis" is an intolerable paradox, but invoking "real crisis" as a moment of radical change can obscure the processes, practices, and continuities undergirding anything like a revolutionary shift. This is a simple point, but it introduces the difficult question of how processes of substantial and salutary political breakthroughs are possible, how they ever have been, and whether they could ever be again.

For all the talk of crises—economic crisis, constitutional crisis, climate crisis, healthcare crisis, or as has become common, polycrisis—crisis commentary is almost never an invitation to a dramatic conjunctural shift. More often than not, as Hall and his colleagues made clear over four decades ago, crisis talk transmuted into "moral panic" becomes a pretext for a ruling class to enforce brutal order, reliably along racialized class lines.

Feminist philosopher Eva von Redecker captures the dilemma succinctly:

> A kind of "background certainty" has emerged: We are aware that our form of life is running out of resources and that we are caught up in the catastrophic dynamic of climate change. However, this is more often articulated in the form of an apocalyptic expectation of doom than in revolutionary hope.

Von Redecker's point is not that we simply need a different, more hopeful attitude but that material conditions and structures of power consistently render the emergence of serious liberatory practices and breakthroughs hard if not impossible to develop, and the shift from radical experiments to a lasting shift in political paradigms harder still.

In turn, I find it somewhat naive when leftists—and I'll admit that I've done this myself—point to increased policing and draconian "crisis" policies as a sign that our political and economic system is in dire straits and is thus resorting to desperate measures.

We must avoid vulgar crisis determinism. Authoritarian state powers, lashing out as if they're in their final throes, are not therefore on the verge of collapse. It is nonetheless common to posit that the extent of state repression faced by a social movement reflects a state that perceives itself as under threat. Maybe that's true—I'd never underestimate the paranoiac responses of those with power, to which they jealously cling. But it seems just as likely that a violent power system, forged in domination, is primed to foster more violent practices over time, and not only as a point of necessity to maintain the dominant order but as a form of habit. There can be, as Indian Marxist historian Ranajit Guha has illustrated, "dominance without hegemony," power structures operating not through the persuasion of bourgeois cultural hegemony but through the dominant coercion of the colonizer over the colonized.

The nuclear, US-backed state of Israel was not put under existential threat by the attacks of October 7, for example; yes, its supposedly inviolable security infrastructure was ruptured, but the state's existence was by no means at risk. Indeed, the rhetorical demand that Israel be seen as both consistently imperiled and undefeatable at the same time has grounded its ability to carry out a genocide. Israel's accelerated annihilation of Gaza spoke as much to a nation-state in the long practice of obliterating Palestinian lives as it did to a country responding with furious desperation to a perceived moment of crisis.

More to the point, even if extreme state repression is sometimes a desperate, flailing response to a crisis of authority, what does that matter if the state's ability to produce such violent, crushing responses is itself not at risk? What does it mean to speak of crisis in such a scenario?

As von Redecker points out, it's not at all self-evident that "times of great uncertainty are also always times of the greatest creativity." Instead, "the opposite would be far more plausible: structures that have gone off the rails lead to paralysis and impotence or reduce the actors' repertoire to a few basic patterns of action that are particularly well anchored." Meanwhile, police and military forces can rely on their own well-anchored practices; they know how to beat, kidnap, and shoot.

"A single, isolated rupture rarely has the effect of transforming structures because *standard procedures and sanctions* can usually repair the torn fabric of social practice," von Redecker writes (emphasis mine). She doesn't foreclose revolutionary change, though, because it is under the same constraints that such change has happened before, "when a sequence of interrelated ruptures disarticulates the previous structural network, makes repair difficult, and makes a novel rearticulation possible." Even then, and such a constellation is rare and hard enough, lasting change for the better is not assured.

BERLANT, the theorist of "crisis ordinariness," died of cancer in June 2021, aged sixty-three, in the second year of the global

Covid-19 pandemic; the Covid death toll at that point in the US was, by some estimates, close to one million. The first year of the pandemic, especially its earliest months, demanded and deserved a framework of crisis that was anything but ordinary—this was a temporality of crisis-as-rupture requiring previously unimagined responses on a planetary scale, and fast. This was crisis-as-continuity, too, as the preexisting fault lines of race, class and nationality determined which communities would suffer the worst of the virus's consequences. Anthropologist Carolyn M. Rouse pointed out at the time that biopolitical systems of regulatory control—stay-at-home orders, testing and mask mandates, social distancing—were ostensibly set up for the benefit of everyone but primarily served the health and well-being of the more privileged members of US society. Millions of poor and working class Black people and other marginalized groups were subjected, meanwhile, to a necropolitical governance of exposure to death and debilitation (overcrowded work environments and living conditions, houselessness, packed prisons, continued police violence).

"The virus has exposed how people, living side by side, can have radically different experiences with state and institutional power," wrote Rouse, emphasizing the "fault lines between a biopolitical system set up to care for whites and a necropolitical system that treats Black bodies as expendable, useful only for labor." It did not have to be this way. For a brief period, the recognition and determination of a global pandemic crisis suggested the possibility of a better way through.

In 2021, the *New York Times* published a series reflecting on the pandemic's first year, titled "The Year Our Reality Broke." And in 2021, this indeed felt a more accurate description of that world historical time, in which new "horizons of expectation" (to borrow Koselleck's phrase) still looked vast and open. It feels like a lifetime ago.

In the *Times* series, journalist Rachel Cohen wrote, "Across the country, all levels of government put in place policies that just a few months earlier would have been seen by most people—not to mention most politicians—as radical and politically naïve." Cohen listed eviction moratoria, pauses to student debt payments, stimulus checks, decarceration efforts, car-free street plans, significantly expanded benefits.

"Historically, pandemics have forced humans to break with the past and imagine their world anew. This one is no different. It is a portal, a gateway between one world and the next," wrote Arundhati Roy in 2020. "We can choose to walk through it, dragging the carcasses of our prejudice and hatred, our avarice, our data banks and dead ideas, our dead rivers and smoky skies behind us. Or we can walk through lightly, with little luggage, ready to imagine another world. And ready to fight for it."

Today, just a few years later, words like Roy's and Cohen's make for bitter reading. The portal led to a mass grave, and then the portal closed. Not one of the cited pandemic provisions remained after spring 2023. The Biden administration was lauded for delivering a strong post-pandemic economy, but it was an economic reality that most Americans could not feel or enjoy. The "glimpses," like debt relief and eviction moratoria, were consigned to crisis time. I wrote as long ago as mid-2020 that "the logic of virus containment has not escaped the logic of capitalism: there's a reason that power will bend in the face of what it sees as a temporary crisis in order to keep capital buoyant in the long term."

The evidence seemed to make abundantly clear what so many already knew prior to the pandemic: that, as philosopher Geoff Mann noted in an April 2020 essay, "the economics that has dominated mainstream knowledge for decades cannot provide a fix for any of this." Mann continued:

> Without considerable work at both the institutional and political-ideological levels, that lesson will not stick, but will instead fit easily into the narrative of a normal temporarily undone by an exogenous "shock."

The lesson did not stick. Instead, states scrambled for short-term fixes along Keynesian lines in order to return to the same "normal", a normal which the need for such interventions had shown to be so lacking.

We got no Green New Deal, no universal basic income, nothing close to universal healthcare; we got instead the limited and compromised investments of Bidenomics, and then even those were swiftly crippled by Trump's embrace of neoliberal authoritarianism. Trump's 2025 tax and spending bill included around $1 trillion in federal cuts to Medicaid and the largest cuts ever to food assistance benefits, funneling $175 billion to fascist border enforcement and, as the *Nation* magazine's John Nichols put it, delivering "the most massive transfer of wealth upward in American history" through tax benefits for the rich.

Austerity politics is always a decision not a necessity. It is also, as Melinda Cooper has pointed out, not even austere: pro-austerity governments since the Nixon administration in the 1970s have overseen lavish public spending in the shape of tax cuts and subsidies for holders of financial wealth (which does not trickle down), as well as funding for policing, prisons and war machines. As Tooze has often pointed out, when Keynes said in 1942 that "anything we can actually do we can afford," he was arguing that sovereign governments have extraordinary capacity to mobilize finances; the constraints lie elsewhere. State economies are not households with checking accounts. Governments issue currency and use fiscal policy to fund programs and wars and to stabilize the economy against runaway inflation. We saw this (and with great benefit to the US economy) in the short-lived pandemic provisions. The limits—what we could "actually do"—were political, technical, material and logistical, and extremely complicated as such, but they were not budgetary. The political limits made themselves all too clear.

Much ink has rightly been spilled over right-wing backlashes to pandemic measures. The viral spread of right-wing conspiracy theorizing played a major role here, shaped by ideologies of individualist liberty pervasive in the conservative American imaginary. Meanwhile, the liberal edict to simply "trust the science" not only alienated millions of people (who already had ample reason to distrust pharmaceutical giants and the healthcare system); it also failed to communicate the uncertainties inherent to scientific research.

Indeed, in a Wittgensteinian framework, efficacious vaccines are to be trusted precisely because they are not held certain—they are posits of knowledge. "If you cannot doubt a thing, you cannot know it," Wittgenstein wrote. As I noted in the introduction, this means is that if you claim to know something, someone can ask you, "How do you know that?" and you can show them evidence, something more convincing than the original proposition you claimed to know. Disagreements about what counts as compelling evidence might arise, but a person who refuses all evidence shows themself incapable or unwilling to engage in the very thing we call knowledge.

"Conspiracists do not actually question authority or expertise, as they often claim; they discount and reject it," writes author and filmmaker Astra Taylor in her recent book *The Age of Insecurity*.

"Real questioning, in contrast, involves genuine curiosity and uncertainty and the acceptance of possibly being wrong." The deadly certainty of committed vaccine denialists, for whom any evidence of millions of lives saved would be a priori rejected, would likely not be shifted by more such evidence. But right-wing efforts to turn masks, vaccines and Covid tests into enemy objects could not have succeeded without the liberal center's treatment of healthcare as a site of individualized rather than societal responsibility.

The same powers that offered temporary concessions at the pandemic's height were also overseeing a system of violent healthcare inequality, both domestically and internationally. Vaccine development and roll out was an unprecedented feat. But at the same time, Western nations, the World Trade Organization and pharmaceutical companies, alongside billionaire intellectual property fetishist Bill Gates, upheld an international vaccine apartheid by refusing to waive intellectual property rules for vaccine development or adequately share knowledge and technology with middle- and low-income countries in desperate need. In the "year our reality broke," some of the worst assumptions of our global political economy held all too steady; "our reality" did not break evenly.

President Biden went on television and declared the pandemic "over" in 2022, at a point when an estimated 400-plus people were still dying from Covid in the US per day, exemplifying what Beatrice Adler-Bolton and Artie Vierkant, authors of *Health Communism*, call "the sociological production of the end of the pandemic." The coronavirus didn't stop spreading and killing, but the government stopped counting and publishing Covid data—a practice that had been so definitive in marking the pandemic's first years as a new reality about which we must gather information, about which we must know.

To counter widespread fear and uncertainty at the height of the pandemic, efforts were made toward producing and signaling knowledge. Deaths and hospitalizations were no doubt under-counted, but they were counted and published as data. This was statistics in the original sense of the word—political arithmetic, data of the state. Yet when politicians and business leaders named the pandemic's end, it was a turn away from activities of knowing and toward a different kind of certainty—the certainty that normality must prevail. "Many countries, including the United States, ramped up tracking efforts at the height of the pandemic," the *New York Times* reported in early 2024. "But they have since been cut back, leaving scientists to guess the scale of respiratory virus infections. Wastewater and hospitalizations can provide clues, but neither is a sensitive measure."

No, the mass death crisis did not "end" with assured knowledge that viral trajectories no longer threatened lives and the health of hundreds of thousands more people. The status of the crisis as "over" instead hinged on the certainties of a political order in which capital is sovereign. Under Biden, investment in future pandemic preparedness was woefully insufficient; the Trump 2.0 regime has, of course, totally kneecapped such research with ferocious funding cuts. It's dizzyingly stupid, but not unreasonable if you're a multibillionaire white supremacist with fantasies of sequestering from future catastrophes in militarized, virus-proofed zones and bunkers.

Recall Roitman's point that the designation of a crisis "is a distinction that secures 'a world' for observation." The Covid crisis secured, for a period and in certain places, a world seemingly (and unequally) more attentive to death and sickness, to our relative vulnerabilities and interdependencies, to the spaces we share and the air we breathe. A world that gestured to recognizing the labor of some of its most exploited workers as "essential." Remember the bourgeois lockdown ritual of banging pots and pans to thank the healthcare workers? Ridiculous at the time, and all the worse for being so fleeting a gesture of recognition. The sociologically produced end to the crisis was a turning away from even that moment of acknowledgement.

The activities of certainty here—the practices of "returning to normal"—worked in opposition to the activities of knowledge gathering and knowledge production that attended the pandemic in its uncertainty-riddled, critical first years. Not only knowledge in terms of pandemic tracing, learning more about Covid's consequences, and preparing for future viruses, but also not-knowing: learning new praxes in our everyday lives to provide for each other and support our neighbors through mutual aid networks; the not-knowing and learning to find each other. By bracketing the mass death event of Covid into a crisis/noncrisis temporality, the state confined to "crisis time" those emergent challenges to the hegemonic economic common sense—small but crucial challenges, like the widespread communal care efforts that gestured to the possibility of more collective forms of life.

"The representation of crisis and the rhetoric it organizes always have at least this purpose: to determine, in order to limit it, a more serious and more formless threat, one which is in fact faceless and normless," writes Jacques Derrida on economic recession in the 1980s. "By determining it as crisis, one tames it, domesticates it, neutralizes it." There is a taming function to upholding the crisis/normality dyad. Theorist Didier Fassin notes that crisis narratives can funnel mass collective uncertainty into a more recognizable frame of sense making—(*it's okay, this isn't normal, this is a crisis, and so it will end*)—and that we must thus be attentive to "who has the authority to articulate the existence of a crisis, and who does not, and what this diagnosis authorizes, and with which purposes."

As the "end" of the Covid crisis made clear, demarcations of historical times of crisis are not objectively imposed, and certainly not democratically decided. In the case of the pandemic, crisis talk and the temporalities it ordered did the work of enabling and also foreclosing unprecedented political economic shifts; a terrifying historic moment that made extraordinary, long-lasting change appear—briefly—possible. And then not.

In the over half-decade since the US government decided that the Covid crisis was over, we have been subjected to a full-scale assault on knowledge production. If the designation "crisis" secures a world for observation, Donald Trump's regime has committed itself to making even critical acts of observation impossible. This is, of course, no embrace of a normless threat to the status quo; it is fascism.

Within days of coming to power for a second time, Trump's administration pulled offline many thousands of government webpages. Datasets from the Center for Disease Control, including the social vulnerability index and environmental justice index used to quantify disproportionate health risks among particular demographics, were taken down, along with countless other federal agency datasets relating to pandemic research, bird flu, HIV, reproductive health and more. It was a ferocious purge that left scientists, researchers and activists scrambling to archive the pages and preserve the data.

The far-reaching information removal was, according to Trump's federal lackeys, to ensure that all government sites complied with the White House's new executive orders. Then came the all-out onslaught on science funding, relentless attacks on higher education through a tidal wave of obscene funding cuts, the vile weaponization of antisemitism accusations to defund schools and attack scholars, and the gutting of any government agency committed to researching health and environmental realities. The Trump administration removed exhibits about slavery, LBGTQ+ struggles, and labor history from National Parks and monuments. In response to disappointing jobs reports in mid-2025, Trump called the accurate statistics "phony" and fired the Bureau of Labor Statistics commissioner.

Trump's administration cut billions in federal grants to science agencies and universities; money has been withheld from research proposals found, in some frenzied cursory keyword search, to fall outside the Trumpian taxonomy. Forbidden terms that could lead to funding removal included women, disability, bias, status, trauma, Black, and Hispanic communities, as well as socioeconomic, ethnicity and systemic. Trump's information purge is an ideological, base-baiting assault on diversity and higher education, and a choreographed narrative of revenge against the liberal establishment that will primarily harm the working class. The collateral damage includes setbacks to cancer research, lowered capacity to prepare for extreme weather events, and major reductions in already pitiful pandemic preparedness efforts.

The mass firings and enormous funding cuts constituted a bloodless coup, promising millions more premature deaths and rampant illnesses in the future. The expungement of thousands of pages of government data and decimation of research and healthcare funding, though, like the sociological production of the end of the pandemic, do not simply produce terrifying uncertainty. These were acts of certainty against knowledge. The aim for today's authoritarians is to produce an epistemic terrain in which, in the absence of knowledge, there is a huge amount of fearful uncertainty, yes—but an uncertainty hitched to the hardening of bedrock fascist certainties.

In a 2025 interview, the least-educated US education secretary in history, Linda McMahon, said that she believes it is time for Americans to question the necessity of four-year college degrees for most students. The irony, of course, is that the US university system is anything but the radical hub of communization that its Republican opponents suggest. The neoliberalized university has in recent decades been a machine for turning young people into indebted human capital, relying on precarious adjunct labor and overseen by top-heavy administrations and corporate trustees. The university as a structure has been a gift to capital's interests far more than it has produced a generation of left-wing agitators. Four-year college degrees have never been a great equalizer, but their destruction helps ensure the right-wing fantasy of an uneducated underclass.

The decimation of the university and college system is an economic own goal for the US, but such is the mark of an administration committed to producing an ever more unequal, sicker, poorer country, so long as it is organized around white supremacy and privatization. The administration celebrated cuts to the National Institute of Health for saving $500 billion in federal spending over the next twenty-five years. In fact, economists David Cutler and Ed Glaeser estimate the cuts will lead to over $8 trillion in losses.

With each gut-wrenching announcement of the latest move to thwart interdependent flourishing, it is tempting, and by no means incorrect, to speak of multiple crises made gravely worse under fascist rule. To yield to this temptation, however, would be to miss the ways authoritarian attacks on knowledge obviate crisis narratives in the worst of ways: There can be no crisis if fascist rule silences all pushback. Then the problem is not a political order in crisis but a fascist order of ever greater suffering, without opposition.

This does not mean, though, that robust knowledge production, accurate data, fact-finding and fact-checking are necessarily antifascist activities. But again, in this terrifying time, it is not our doubts but the world-ordering certainty of the ruling class, made manifest in their actions as much as their words, that is the greater problem at hand.

When, in 2022, the historian Tooze wrote a column in the *Financial Times* titled "Welcome to the Age of Polycrisis," it was to signal that there was something new here—a new intractability and complexity in this epoch of globalized financial capitalism, networked interconnectedness and surveillance, violent inequality and exploitative interdependence, environmental decimation, global pandemic, economic shocks, rising far-right forces and fierce geopolitical antagonisms. "The shocks are disparate, but they interact so that the whole is even more overwhelming than the sum of the parts. At times one feels as if one is losing one's sense of reality," wrote Tooze. With "polycrisis," at least we have a label for why we often can't seem to think beyond these entangled crises, for why no one set of solutions appears available to deliver the world and its inhabitants from catastrophe. To repeat what Hont writes of "crisis" in modern usage, "polycrisis" is all the more "an indicator of both the intensity of a crisis and the perception of it as such."

In a follow-up newsletter, Tooze noted that "both the fact that we have every reason to think that we are at a dramatic threshold point, but also that our need to reach for a term as unspecific as polycrisis indicates our flailing inability to grasp our situation with the confidence and conceptual clarity that we might once have hoped for." Such confusion is, as Tooze is the first to admit, the observing analyst's privilege. The harms produced at the interstices of a polycrisis—such lived realities as incarceration, homelessness, poverty, eviction, mass displacement, white supremacist violence, loss of medical care, illness, famine, war, and genocide—are immediately felt; lack of conceptual clarity is not the problem for victims of this necropolitical order. If the climate crisis is a crisis for us all, if global pandemics are a crisis for us all, they are not equally distributed as such, nor equally produced.

As the philosopher Olúfẹ́mi O. Táíwò notes in his call for reparative climate justice, the accumulated advantages and disadvantages of five hundred years of "global racial empire" continue to determine the organization of planetary crises. For the billions of people who have, without repair, accumulated the disadvantages of colonialism and its racial capitalist afterlives—those now on the frontlines of ecocide—what could it mean to speak of the epochal difference made by an age of polycrisis, as opposed to stubborn, worsening violent continuities? That's not to pretend, however, that those of us invested in forging liberatory countercurrents can somehow ignore the complexity of the systems in which, and beyond which, we collectively seek change.

To stipulate a state of polycrisis is, at the very least, to recognize and insist that no one crisis-segment can be isolated and addressed alone. But that's not so new either—as noted above, Hall, among others, stressed that all crises are overdetermined, are never just economic. Hall's very notion of conjunctural analysis relied on understanding crisis as a complex phenomenon, resistant to reduction—a point Tooze has also well noted. So, whether it is appropriate or useful to speak of a new era of mass, convergent crises is somewhat of an academic question, unless the answer informs how we go forward—unless the novelty of the era's crisis formations requires new kinds of action and analysis in response. This is among Tooze's reasons for championing the "polycrisis" designation: that we not, as Marx warned, "present this new scene in world history in time-honored disguise" and conjure only "spirits of the past to [our] service."

Central to the problem of polycrisis, though, is that with such a focus on complexity, it can struggle to "present," or represent, this "new scene" at all, let alone in time-honored disguise. "For the moment and in our current historical situation, a sense of history can only be reawakened by a Utopian vision lying beyond the horizon of our current globalized system, which appears too complex for representation in thought," wrote Fredric Jameson in 2015. The headily abstracted nature of finance capital—exemplified, Jameson argued, in the derivative, that bizarre, future-looking yet temporally myopic bet-upon-a-bet—sees possible futures narrativized by world leaders (of state and capital) in terms of immensely complicated risks, and almost never more liberatory doubts.

Yet if the language game of crisis, as Roitman reminds us, produces meaning in making visible some things and invisible others, the language game of polycrisis—in its necessary and only sometimes useful abstraction—risks making invisible some of the clearest terrains of struggle directly in front of us: the narrative of polycrisis is paralyzing in the way any bird's-eye view on the planetary condition would be. There's a tendency for theorists of polycrisis to lean toward technocratic solutions, because the worlds made visible in narratives of polycrisis consist in the objects of technocracy—unfathomably complex networks, supply chains, trade deficits, billions of people all too configured as human capital or surplus, financial instruments, political authorities, predictive models, and the like, requiring of vast overviews and expert administration.

We should not close our eyes to these complex systems. They are, after all, a key articulation of how power functions and finds representation in this conjuncture. But nor should we pretend that we are thus left without any direction for shared struggle across territories and against all too entrenched currents of historic oppression (certainties, that is).

Philosopher John Dewey's anti-technocratic dictum that "the man who wears the shoe knows best that it pinches and where it pinches" is not an argument against conjunctural thinking, and "polycrisis" really does capture problems of massive scope. But we should be wary of crisis narratives without agents and activities, descriptions that occlude embodied social knowledges and practices. If today's crises appear permanent and inescapable, as they truly can, we must not forget that they were produced over decades of aggregate activities, policies, violences, norms, and habits. I'm also not suggesting that polycritical analysis demands only technocratic managerialism as response—the term can be and has been used to evidence the need for radical political interventions and experimentation. But in the world-picture projected through a framework of polycrisis, decisive change is almost always understood to come only from existing seats of power.

Narratives of polycrisis tend to delineate problems of knowledge in the face of complexity—that everything is just too entangled, too unprecedented, that, as Tooze has put it, "if you think you have 'figured it out,' you are not experiencing polycrisis." And from the point of view of global policymaking, who could argue with that? But such an admission doesn't tell us too much about the fabric, texture, experience of the material reality polycrisis supposedly captures.

It's notable that in 2025, Tooze reflected that "as a description of the general scene, 'polycrisis' no longer seems so apt," noting that, compared to when the term gained traction a few years prior, "in many ways and in some places the situation today is more extreme." He stressed that the concept of polycrisis can only be useful if understood as perspectival; a term that's useful for, say, the World Bank when making its annual list of "fragile and conflict-affected situations" for its own purposes is not necessarily a helpful analytic to for those who need to navigate intersecting catastrophes and violences on the ground. A crisis, recognized, named and faced from the point of view of survival, or liberatory struggle, is not necessarily a problem of having insufficient knowledge for "figuring it out."

We might know that current conditions are intolerable and unsustainable for collective flourishing and know *that* these are circumstances of compounding complexity; the representatives of state and capitalist power, meanwhile, can rely instead on *know-how*. I do not mean they possess superior cunning or insight, quite the opposite; rather, I mean know-how in the way Wittgenstein, in his *Philosophical Investigations*, describes a child coming to understand how to follow a rule, like continuing a mathematical series (to continue to "add two," for example to "2, 4, 6, 8 . . .") The circumstances in which the child is said to understand, and thus know, the rule, are simply the child's ability, once trained, to go on adding two in this context when asked to do so. It is an embodied practice, not manifest in the description of some internal mental process akin to "Eureka! I see it in my mind's eye, 'x + 2'!"—that would be meaningless without the actual carrying-on of the series in practice that constitutes understanding.

"Ask yourself: in what sort of case, in what kind of circumstances, do we say, 'Now I know how to go on'?" Wittgenstein asks in his exploration of rule-following and understanding. According to philosopher Rupert Read, Wittgenstein shows the "profound grammatical difference between know-how and knowledge-that . . . undercutting the currently popular project of reduction of the former to the latter." I leave it to Wittgenstein scholars to debate the specifics of his distinction. It is useful for us here, though, to appreciate that our understanding of our conjuncture in terms of *knowing that* certain conditions of entangled crisis pertain does not translate to *knowing how* to "go on" in a new direction. It is far, far easier for those with power to simply continue the series. Yet it is not by virtue of some Eureka realization or vision or complex synthesis that liberatory know-how will be attained.

We must not be distracted from the ways power is also *not* complex. Like a white former marine choking an unhoused, distressed Black man to death on a full New York City subway car in the name of public safety. Like ICE agents chasing farmworkers through fields and shooting civilian observers in the face. Like politicians voting to spend billions in wealth transfers to the richest through tax cuts while cutting Medicaid and food stamps. Like billionaire tech moguls building data centers the size of Manhattan to use up more water and energy than entire small nation-states to fuel an AI-drenched future we have not chosen. Like cops pummeling students protesting genocide. Like genocide.

There is every reason to reject permanent crisis (and crisis management) for those who are tortured, killed, imprisoned, exploited, and left to die in their millions in service of this "normality." Nor need we frame "crisis" as a rupture in historical time (a quasi-religious telos) in order to take critical action. To speak of crisis *can* be an invocation to collective activity—territorially situated, durational, embodied—toward more flourishing shared forms of life. But these activities are almost never expressed in the grammar of resolving a crisis as viewed like a puzzle from above. They are, rather, part of the work of knowing-how to go on, in forms of life forged against the goings-on of fascist power and capitalist accumulation. How to not go on like this.

With what sort of practices of refusal, strike, blockade, learning, sharing, escape, redistribution, boycott, survival, and collective care do we know *how* to go on, and on?

2
Border Certainties

> *. . . It takes*
> *Time, lots of people's time, to organize*
> *The world this way. & violence. It takes more*
> *Violence. Violence no one can confuse for*
> *Anything but violence. So much violence*
> *Changes relationships, births a people*
> *They can reason with.*
>
> Wendy Trevino, "Brazilian Is Not a Race, 16"

I'LL NEVER forget the words of Democratic policy advisor Cecilia Muñoz, once a key figure behind President Barack Obama's immigration enforcement policies: "There are policy choices to be made about who should be an immigrant, and that includes removing folks who don't qualify under the law," she said in a 2021 interview. "That's, I think, just the reality of being a nation." Her comment struck me and stayed with me precisely because she *appeared* to be saying almost nothing.

Muñoz's words seemed true in the same way "all bachelors are unmarried men" is true—analytically, by virtue of the meaning of its constituent terms. The advisor was offering little more than a definition: when "a nation" is constituted as the Westphalian nation-state, defined by its borders and the inclusions and exclusions they entail, which are legitimized by "the law," then determining who is or is not "an immigrant," and who should be removed, is indeed the "reality" of being a nation.

My point, though, is that statements like Muñoz's are question begging, because they treat the terms by which nation-states order the movement or immobility of people over the earth as fixed and mutually entailing—certain. With definitions held static, sedimented through historic processes, Muñoz is saying nothing more than "the state's gonna state." But that's saying a lot, too. In other words, "the reality of being a nation" is excluding and "removing folks."

You can't find evidence to prove false an analytic truth; for example, you'd have to change the meaning of the term "bachelor" (in its common usage) to ever find evidence of a bachelor who is not an unmarried man. If a married man started identifying himself as a bachelor, you'd either presume he was joking, or that he didn't know what the word "bachelor" meant. It's a trivial thought experiment to imagine a world where etymologies took different turns over time, in which, perhaps, the word "bachelor" never came into being, or garnered a different meaning. It's an ethical imperative, meanwhile, to reckon with the terms of entrenched assumptions around borders and migration. That Muñoz's statement appeared to her as obvious, seemingly true by the meaning of its terms alone and thus beyond challenge, reflects how dangerously certain we have come to hold the bordered, exclusionary nation-state as a world-ordering assemblage, even with knowledge of its comparatively recent formation in the scope of world history.

And to what end? Compared to Donald Trump's relentless racist assault on immigrants and extraordinary expansion of the US's already fearsome deportation machine, Muñoz's bland, definitional gesture seems anodyne. Trump's official White House social media accounts have posted meme-ified videos of chained men being sent to a gulag in El Salvador; official Trump 2024 election signs bore the slogan "Mass Deportation Now!"; the president and his loyalists celebrated building a concentration camp in the Florida Everglades because it was surrounded by deadly alligators and pythons; they dubbed the camp "Alligator Alcatraz," immediately sold merchandise, and publicly guffawed at the thought of desperate displaced people getting eaten by alligators should they try to escape the camp. "I voted for this!" thousands of users with MAGA-themed profiles posted on social media, in response to videos of immigrant workers being dragged away by masked ICE brownshirts.

But Trump and other border fascists have not gained ground in a vacuum; their brutality emerged in a context in which border regimes have been established as a certainty of governance. If modern state formations are relatively recent, the idea that the nation is defined by a "secure" border is newer still, but just as entrenched.

The current postures of US and most Western political leaders can be very roughly sketched in terms of empowered white nationalist reaction and the ill-thought scramblings of a conservative liberal center, bending evermore rightwards—particularly when it comes to upholding the narrative that migration is a problem, that there is a migration or border crisis, and that this is a crisis faced by powerful nation-states in the Global North. The border in these discussions is never limited to a physical border but is an entire architecture determining the movement or stasis of human beings through bureaucracy, surveillance, categorization, policing, incarceration, and expulsion in operations stretching the entire expanse of the nation-state and beyond (for example in the use of extraterritorial detention camps).

Only forty years ago, the militarized border was not settled—or at least not on the same terms as today. The editorial position of the conservative *Wall Street Journal* went as far as to call for a US Constitutional amendment consisting of only five words: "There shall be open borders." This was not an embrace of sharing land and resources but a push for the free movement of trade and cheap labor to advantage capitalism; it was a position the paper's editorial board reaffirmed in 2000. Now, such a demand is considered the preserve of only the radical left.

Of course, violent state acts of nativist anti-immigrant exclusion and bordering run through US history but the idea that migration per se is an existential threat to the nation-state, which needs an expansive border regime, is relatively recent. As journalist John Washington points out in his book *The Case for Open Borders*, for the first century of the United States' existence as a nation, it had no federal immigration laws; up until the 1990s, there was no significant border infrastructure along the US-Mexico border. US Immigration and Customs Enforcement, or ICE, was only founded in 2003. In 2025, it became by far the highest-funded law enforcement agency in the federal government.

In just a few short decades, the call for open borders has become so illegible to mainstream establishment politics that now the Trumpian right can call any policy that doesn't shutter the US-Mexico border and round up immigrants en masse an "open border" approach. How could a paradigm shift so dramatically in such a relatively short period? Historian Quinn Slobodian has explored the willingness of the libertarian right to turn against the free movement of people once it was understood that borderless capital could be better served by heavily policing immigration as a method to cheapen labor. The hardened border is, in fact, a spatial fix for capital, with the benefit of segmenting international labor.

This is a point that scholar of border regimes Harsha Walia has long stressed—capital requires "immobilized" labor, which the border provides. As Slobodian puts it, "When we see neoliberalism as a project of retooling the state to save capitalism, then its supposed opposition to the populism of the Right begins to dissolve." While certain market conservatives not too long ago may have advocated for a form of "open borders," they did so from a conviction in the necessity of the capitalist order. If the hardened border is a somewhat new mainstream political consensus, it sits atop an older ideological bedrock of propertization, dominion, conquest and control.

So, what type of certainty does today's border regime inhabit? How is that certainty articulated and regulated through mainstream political discourse? I will argue that border rule, border "security," relies on a property logic that functions as a certainty in the broadly Wittgensteinian sense: a hinge around which our political practices turn, but one that is itself not grounded in deeper justification. Like all the most dangerous types of certainties, these regimes are contingent arrangements, taken as foundational and natural; they have relied and will always rely upon continued violence and oppression to remain in place. We will see once again how the language of uncertainty has been consistently misleading when applied to questions of the border. The problem lies in border rule as a certainty, and the specific type of inculcated certainty that it is.

IT MIGHT SEEM immediately strange to talk of border rule as a certainty, given that popular discourse around borders and immigration reliably focuses on the border's insecurity. But narratives of border insecurity, border and migration crises, and immigrants as producing social and political uncertainties (rather than being the subjects experiencing uncertainty themselves) reveal what is held fast.

Far-right leaders make no secret about what they believe border security is for and thus what it means to secure a border: to shore up white standing, emboldened in this moment of white chauvinist backlash against the antiracist, feminist movements of the preceding years, and as a reliable scapegoat for working-class economic pain. "Secure" as in the key verb in the notorious Fourteen Words, the best-known white supremacist phrase in the English language: "We must secure the existence of our people and a future for white children."

"That we live in a world that opposes security to health, life, and creativity couldn't be clearer," notes writer and psychoanalyst Akshi Singh in *Parapraxis* magazine. The right-wing project of palingenetic nationalism is clear in its intent. The idea that immigration is something to be secured against is not, however, the preserve of white nationalists. As Singh puts it, "Security is the shared shibboleth that can't be questioned, much like borders." Democrats may express horror at the excesses of Trump's deportation machine, but the entire political establishment in the US, and most of the West, has come to take securocratic border rule as a given.

Take, for an illustrative example, the only televised debate between Donald Trump and Kamala Harris prior to the 2024 elections. Trump spewed reliably racist and lie-riddled diatribes about Haitian immigrants eating pets and towns being taken over by "millions of people pouring into our country from prisons and jails, from mental institutions and insane asylums." David Muir, the ABC news anchor and presidential debate moderator, opened the discussion on immigration with a lengthy question posed to Harris. "We know that illegal border crossings reached a record high in the Biden administration," he said, noting that, since President Joe Biden "imposed tough asylum restrictions," the crossing numbers were down. "Why did the administration wait until six months before the election to act?" he asked.

Consider the tangled knot of assumptions required for such a question to seem a natural, reasonable one to pose. For one, it presupposed that these border crossings were necessarily a problem for the country. Muir's question also assumed that since the crossings were "illegal" they should be thought of as bad occurrences that needed to be stopped. The fact that the criminalization of migration *creates* these very categories of illegality was wholly ignored. "We know that illegal border crossings reached a record high," he said—an interesting use of the word "know" in a sentence so loaded but involving so little relevant information. What we actually know, when it comes to most of the cases Muir was referring to, is that these crossings were made almost entirely by people who entered the US through the Southern border in order to *seek* legal status and protections. The fact that the very same border crossings could be deemed legal with an act of recategorization under law—and are, in fact, legal in many cases according to international human rights law on asylum seeking—is also pushed from the frame of legibility. Thirdly, Muir's question to Harris took for granted that tough asylum restrictions were the only reasonable response to the high number of border crossings. Muir did not ask about the justifiability of Biden's tough asylum restrictions, merely their timing; why not sooner?

Harris, like Biden before her, and most every centrist Democrat in living memory, wholly accepted the premises. Albeit in the predictably moderated tones of a Democratic border authoritarian, she upheld the right-wing lie that immigration should be stopped. "The United States Congress, including some of the most conservative members of the United States Senate, came up with a border security bill which I supported," she said. Let it never be forgotten that Democrats in 2024 campaigned on Republican talking points, with Harris donning khaki for photo ops at the Arizona border wall, flanked by border patrol officers. The narrative of a "border crisis" was taken for granted from the jump, in turn further cementing the militarized border as beyond challenge.

Trump's fascist escalation, therefore, was constructed upon foundations built as much by Democrats as Republicans. The Biden-Harris administration was not simply borrowing Republican talking points to appeal to conservatives voters. Harsh border policies have been the standard of Democratic administrations for at least three decades. When Bill Clinton signed the 1994 North American Free Trade Agreement to ensure the free movement of capital, the Army Corps of Engineers fenced the US-Mexico border to prevent the entry of the very people the neoliberal trade deal would devastate and displace. Clinton's 1996 immigration laws significantly expanded the United States' ability to detain and deport migrants who had even minor criminal convictions. President Obama relied on the racist, classist narrative of only targeting "criminal" migrants and deported some three million people, earning the moniker "deporter-in-chief."

Trump immediately took advantage of and played upon the figuration of the "criminal" migrant to treat all undocumented people (and many documented immigrants, too) as criminals worthy of gestapo-style ICE roundups. In March 2025, the vast majority of the first two hundred men kidnapped by ICE and sent to an El Salvadorian gulag on groundless claims of gang membership had no criminal record. Many just had tattoos and the relevant race and class backgrounds for targeting. To be clear: the potentially permanent removal to a totalitarian prison camp would not be justified even if every detainee were convicted of serious crimes. But it takes an extraordinary amount of unwarranted faith in—or blindness to—our immigration system and criminal legal system to imagine they produce any sort of moral taxonomy dividing people into deserving innocents and allegedly undeserving "illegal" immigrants.

This was, however, the unchallenged world-picture painted by most every mainstream politician and media outlet. Public opinion, the pollsters and reporters stressed, doesn't like immigration. The polls have spoken!

Within six months of Trump rolling out his deportation program, as each day brought new footage of brutal ICE kidnappings, a Gallup poll found that only 30 percent of US adults believed immigration levels should be reduced. The year prior, 55 percent, nearly double the number of respondents, wanted reduced immigration. Yes, the dramatic shift no doubt reflected a rightful recoiling at the reality of Trump's project in action. It's also likely relevant that once Trump returned to power, Democrats and liberal pundits shifted their focus (albeit fanglessly) to decrying the Trump administration. The unpopularity of Trump's excesses should not, however, be confused with an openness—across the mainstream political spectrum—to challenging the securocratic border paradigm. Even the social democratic Senator Bernie Sanders, while lambasting Trump's mass deportations, expressed agreement with "making sure our borders are stronger."

When a bipartisan coalition of US politicians invokes the need for a *secure* border to fend off a *crisis*, what does this do? In practice, the designations regulate political discourse. According to a speaker's political tendencies, there should either be more arrests, violence, barbed wire, concrete, gulags, and removal or, in the liberal case, some moderate leniency, paths to citizenship, and tolerance at best. Of course, given these options, only the latter is supportable. But the idea that there is, in fact, no need to "secure" the border is rendered unspeakable.

From an electoral point of view, centrists bending rightward have in the last decade only served to strengthen far-right leaders and parties, from Italy to France to Germany, and, of course, to the twice Trump-led US. If liberals continue reaffirming claims that the arrival of displaced people is some sort of crisis *for the nation-state*, the far right will continue to win. Even if validating nationalist angst were a winning strategy for liberals—and it is not—such victories are deals with the devil. In a world where the number of displaced people is inexorably rising from conflict, poverty and climate decimation, we will have only one of two options when it comes to mass migration: opening borders or using mass slaughter as deterrence. There's no contradiction in fighting to end the causes of mass displacement and ensuring the safety of displaced people; shuttering borders does neither.

"THE PROPOSITIONS which one comes back to again and again as if bewitched—these I should like to expunge from philosophical language," Wittgenstein laments in *On Certainty*. I feel the same way about propositions in our political language around border security and migration crises. As anthropologist Roitman reminds us, "crisis" allows "certain questions to be asked while others are foreclosed." Questions like Muir's in the presidential debate, which typify how immigration is discussed as a political challenge, are a part of a crisis discourse that abundantly affirms Roitman's point that crisis functions as a blind spot.

It can't be stressed enough that the crisis in immigration discourse does not reflect reality. Or, more precisely, it does not reflect the realities that it purports to capture; it does, however, reflect a psychic terrain structured around colonial expectations as settled and certain. This "common sense" is simply untrue. Rhetoric in the US and Europe, from the far right to the liberal center, might lead one to believe that the weight of global migration is bearing down on the Global North. It is not.

When reporting on migration, I have emphasized that every so-called border or migrant crisis is, in fact, a crisis for the humans forced to navigate borders. It should make little sense that a powerful nation-state is designated the subject facing a crisis of migration, when it's so clearly displaced people who are in critical circumstances. When news outlets and politicians talk without qualification about a migration or border crisis in the US, Britain or the EU, suggesting that the state faces uncertainty by virtue of new inhabitants, they draw a most violent equivalence between the alleged crisis facing the wealthy countries to which people migrate and the crisis and profound uncertainty faced by those seeking safety and less suffering.

There is a host of reasons, none of them good, as to why typical immigration news coverage so readily mislocates the proper subjects of crisis and doubt. Liberals and leftists stand on shaky ground, for example, when they insist that their commitment to border rule is not racist but simply a question of limited state capacity and upholding a rules-based system, as if the rules were natural law. Even for a global superpower, there's no doubt that it takes considerable resources and work to settle and sustain millions of newcomers into a country, but these are questions of priorities not capacities, challenges not crises.

Recall Keynes's famous line that "anything we can actually do we can afford." We saw this in the case of pandemic stimulus spending; we saw this, too, in the US sending over $20 billion in military aid to Israel for its genocide in the two years following October 7, 2023, or the $8 trillion spent on the so-called War on Terror. According to the Department of Housing and Urban Development, it would cost $20 billion to end homelessness in the

US. The money sent to Israel's war machine was not sitting around, waiting to otherwise be spent on housing and feeding people. Again, nation-state economies are not household budgets, and austerity politics are always a decision, not a necessity.

What have recent US governments decided they can actually do in terms of immigration policy? Since the creation of the Department of Homeland Security in 2003, the federal government has spent an estimated $409 billion on immigration enforcement agencies alone, and tens of billions more on deterrence strategies like barriers and walls. President Trump's latest mass deportation plan is estimated by the libertarian Cato Institute to have a fiscal cost of up to $1 trillion over a decade. And the losses? Due to the loss of workers across US industries, the American Immigration Council found that mass deportation would reduce the US gross domestic product by 4.2 to 6.8 percent. Prioritizing the flourishing of our collective lives, including the lives of those who newly enter the country, rather than securing the border through militarized violence, would see such sums better spent. The $45 billion budgeted for ICE detention centers? That's nearly four times the $12.8 billion the US spent on new affordable housing in 2023. A yearly deportation budget of $88 billion could instead pay for building over 2.9 million houses and 40,000 schools.

But even as things stand right now, even without significant shifts in spending, typical economic arguments against immigration—that it is a burden on taxpayers, draining scant state resources—don't hold water. A major EU-funded study in 2019 found that "in the European countries which host the majority of EU migrants, these households are a net benefit to the public purse." Equally, a comprehensive study on the integration of asylum seekers into the German labor market since 2014 found "no clear correlation between access to the labour market and the number of asylum applications a country received." Nonetheless, Germany's former Chancellor Angela Merkel's extremely reasonable, ethically imperative decision to (albeit too briefly) open her country's doors to refugees in 2015 is treated as a historic misstep. The real reasons for economic hardship for Germany's working class include structural economic problems of postindustrialization, stagnation and contraction, and austerity policies. Since reunification and West Germany's lightning-fast program of radical privatization in the East, the former GDR has faced particular devastation, unemployment and abandonment. Immigrants have caused precisely none of the conditions, and do not, in fact, exacerbate them. The so-called migrant crisis of 2015 has been found in study after study to have had a net positive result on the German economy.

Or take the case of Springfield, Ohio. The arrival of 15,000 asylum seekers from Haiti beginning around 2017 reinvigorated the depressed former manufacturing hub, revived abandoned neighborhoods, replenished a depleted workforce, and drove wage growth. This wasn't enough to stem nativist reaction, however, especially as local schools and hospitals were not given the state and federal resources to support the town's population re-expansion (again, such withholding of resources is a choice, not a necessity, in the world's wealthiest country). When an eleven-year-old boy was killed after a collision between a schoolbus and a car driven by a Haitian immigrant, neo-Nazis descended on the town to protest. Trump repeated lies that Haitians were eating pets and said they "destroyed" the town. The racist narrative took hold, and the fact that Ohio's Republican governor had credited the arrival of Haitian immigrants with Springfield's "resurgence" was readily forgotten.

In short, the left has plenty of intellectual, factual ammunition to show that anti-immigrant claims about a "migrant crisis" overwhelming resources and stealing jobs are bunk and that resources are not immutably scarce; they are hoarded. We can be clear in asserting that there is no migration crisis for Western countries; what there is, instead, is a class war waged by the rich on the poor and the working class, which keeps international labor disenfranchised, disarticulated, disorganized, and fearful.

But stating the facts (that there is no crisis) will hardly be sufficient to break down the ideological stranglehold that border logics maintain over the political order. "Racism sometimes works as a form of displaced or distorted class politics, but not always," the author Richard Seymour notes in writing about the violent August 2024 white riots against immigrant communities in the UK, which took hold in postindustrial, austerity-ravaged cities and towns. These were not, after all, anti-austerity riots in their explicit content. Masked white pogromists set fire to migrant shelters. A materialist understanding must also attend to the role of white nationalism as an ordering force here, forged through colonial rule and racial capitalism. The far right makes this explicit, while liberals and pro-border leftists give the racism unacknowledged license.

"In the places where we deploy the language and logics of security, the question of an unbearable knowledge is often at stake, a defensiveness at work, a mechanism of standing up straight and not thinking," writes the psychoanalyst Singh. He is referencing the words (first recorded in 2009 by author Jacqueline Rose) of an Israeli human rights activist who said, "At the mention of the word security . . . everyone stands up straight and stops thinking." Israel's so-called security walls, Singh writes, partly function to render Palestinians and the history of the ongoing Nakba invisible: "Proximity, history, responsibility—this is what the walls are in service of denying. This denial, we could argue, is the function of security." And the same can be said for border regimes more broadly.

This is not accidental: Israeli officials and Israeli security and arms companies like Elbit Systems have quite literally shaped US and EU border enforcement, while Israel has received $158 billion in military aid from the US, making it the largest such recipient in history. The expansion of brutal securocratic border regimes within and between these territories has been mutually reinforcing.

"Israel has trained U.S. Customs and Border Protection, Homeland Security officials, and thousands of U.S. law enforcement officers in counter- terrorism and border and perimeter security," according to journalist Todd Miller. "One such program, the Law Enforcement Exchange Program (LEEP) claimed that more than 11,000 U.S. police agents have attended their training courses and conferences." As Miller notes:

> The divisions of the police and military of the nation-state are breaking down and reforming to create an even more powerful force: the crux of homeland security. To express this concept specifically for the U.S.-Mexico divide, journalist Jimmy Johnson coined the phrase "Palestine-Mexico border."

The language of security and crisis deployed throughout this militarized transnational nexus occludes the lived realities of the people who migrate or face forced displacement and occupation.

As I've noted, the Trumpist white nationalists and their international counterparts do not alone constitute the forces holding the exclusionary border as a political certainty today; this requires a far broader agreement, including from those liberals who condemn ICE's terror but embrace a more orderly form of exclusion. Racism and Western chauvinism are also rife among liberals, particularly when it comes to Islamophobia and anti-Arab and anti-Palestinian racism. I want to say, though, that there is another, less blatant anchoring problem in need of addressing: property. This institution gives exclusionary border rule the appearance or feeling of being natural, universal, and justified.

Running through the Western concept of property is the *right* to exclude others from that which one possesses. The right to exclude is, legal scholars agree and the Supreme Court has ruled, "universally held to be a fundamental element of the property right." The further hidden premise, in a world ordered by global racial empire, is that the right to exclude is not held equally.

"What stands fast does so," Wittgenstein reminds us, "not because it is intrinsically obvious or convincing; it is rather held fast by what lies around it." What lies around the border as a world-ordering arrangement? Borders are held firmly in place by the vast arrays of bordering activities in which state powers engage, supported by all too many citizens, and with which the rest of us are forced to comply. Specific borders may be contested, but only within a geopolitical framework that takes the fact of borders as a given. Wars are fought over borders but not over the fact of borders. A question like, "But why does the land *belong* to anyone at all?" is rejected as the sort of naive challenge posed by a child who keeps asking, of any situation, "But why?" At a certain point, the adult may have no *good* answer, no *good* reason, no justification.

"Because it is!" the exasperated adult eventually snaps back. Which is not to say these arrangements *just happen*—nation-states and their borders were birthed in blood and are maintained through the constant exertion of state power and coercion, along with a whole bunch of everyday practices in which many of us must participate to live, work, and travel. It is telling, though, that when the border system is directly questioned, another underlying set of ideological commitments, or unexamined certainties—the presumptions of *exclusive ownership*—jump forth.

The writer Ayesha Siddiqi posted on her Twitter account over a decade ago, "Every border implies the violence of its maintenance." The phrase struck a chord and went swiftly viral, and it has been reposted and reposted consistently in the years since. It also struck a nerve, and a steady stream of dismissive replies snake below the tweet, many along the lines of "I bet you would be mad if someone kicked in your front door" (2022) or "Brain dead quote. Do you have a house with locks on the doors? Do you think locks alone are what prevent people from breaking in to [*sic*] your house, and not the threat of violence in the form of police and prison?" (2024). As if it were somehow obvious, needing no further argumentation, that the state should be thought of as a logical extension of private property, always already facing violent intruders at that, against whom violence is presumed warranted—it's private property, after all!

It would certainly be too simple to describe nation-states, the complex posits of contingent history that they are, as collective group properties. So why speak of property at all as the heart of nation-state border regimes, rather than just speak of divided, sometimes contested sovereign territories in which different property arrangements (privatized, nationalized, common) exist in tension? The reason is that border securitization is so consistently justified by thinking in terms of property. *Don't you lock your door?*

To put it all too sweepingly: Border logic rests on a type of property logic for its justification, and that cannot be divorced from the racial hierarchies in which the concept of modern property and legal subjectivities of ownership developed together. It is as a mode of property thinking that border logic has been able to entrench itself as a certainty far beyond the convictions of white nationalists and into the whole liberal capitalist order. Understanding this does not free us from the grim reality of border regimes or capitalist property regimes, but it should at least give pause to those who act as if there's something essentially justified in upholding exclusionary borders.

What does it mean to say that border logic rests on a type of unjustified property logic? For one, there are historic continuities between feudal, colonial, and capitalist property regimes and modern nation-state formation. Justificatory fairytales of modern nation-state foundations are just that—fairytales. States were not formed on an egalitarian footing, with mythic nations composed of equals (once upon a time) coming together and signing social contracts, respectfully marking out delineated territories of equivalent legal standing. Dispossession, land enclosure, conquest, forced exclusions and inclusions—these were the foundational stuff of nation-states.

I'm not suggesting this is the entire story. States and their borders are far messier assemblages than that. There have, of course, been emancipatory struggles to build or reconstitute nations as sovereign states out of former territories of imperial, colonial, and oppressive rule. The Haitian Revolution, in which enslaved Haitians rose up and won independence from France, is a world-historically inspiring example—for which French colonial, then US neocolonial powers have punished Haiti ever since. Later examples of decolonial struggle for counterhegemonic state formation, like the fight for a free Palestine, do not confer legitimacy on the nation-state model per se, by virtue of representing liberatory ruptures within it. If anything, these struggles make all too clear how violently unequal, and continuous with colonial and settler colonial rule, the system of nation-state formation, bordering, and recognition remains today. The irony that former colonial powers and settler colonialists—the invaders, occupiers, and despoilers—are some of the fiercest enforcers of border rule should be lost on no one.

Borders do not, of course, protect a state as collective property, in the sense that a nation's citizens have some equal, communized ownership and shared ability to access and use the territories and bounties of a land by virtue of excluding others. Borders are evidently no insurance of intranational equality and collective flourishing; that's not what borders do. (If they did, then that would arguably be a justificatory ground for border systems, even while leaving questions of inclusion and exclusion unanswered; but no such justification exists in reality). Instead, border rule protects the nation-state–qua–property only in the sense that border regimes maintain an ongoing "racial regime of ownership," as defined by theorist Brenna Bhandar—that is, a property-personhood regime that emerged in the "legal laboratories" of colonial conquest and settlement, in which "property laws and racial subjectivity developed in relation to one another."

The property interests of citizens that are defended and enforced by border regimes are not (for the vast majority) material in terms of owned land or real estate—multinational corporations and individual billionaires own land and resources with borderless freedom, while citizens in a given county are assured no ownership of its land or physical properties. The real property at stake, or at least imagined to be at stake, is of a different sort. It is a status property, consistent with what legal scholar Cheryl Harris identifies in the concept of "whiteness as property" in her famous 1993 paper—that is, the "racialized privilege that was ratified and legitimated in law as a type of status property," through conquest, Indigenous slaughter, chattel slavery and segregation. In a later paper, Harris writes, "Whiteness as property evolved into a more modern form through the law's ratification of the settled expectations of relative white privilege as a legitimate and natural baseline."

In Du Bois's words from 1926, "Whiteness is ownership of the earth forever and ever, amen." Whiteness is not a fixed racial-ethnic category transmuted into status property; whiteness was constructed as a status property through colonialism's racist and racializing processes (and it continues to be constructed through the afterlives of those processes today). To use Siddiqi's formulation, whiteness implies the violence of its own maintenance. It is by virtue of its status as property that whiteness is fiercely guarded but historically expandable as an institution; groups can be granted the status, like Italian, Irish, and white Jewish people have been. The condition for entry, though, has always been a demonstrated willingness to uphold the oppressive racial regime of exclusion that gave whiteness meaning as a status property in the first place. Beneficiaries of whiteness may tend to share certain skin tones and Anglo-European lineages, but the actual content of whiteness is negative, defined by the exclusion and oppression of those deemed nonwhite. This is the expectation of whiteness, and why it is a status that requires and sanctions so much violence to uphold.

As the author Vicky Osterweil puts it, "Private property is a racial concept, and race, a propertarian one." And this is the sort of property that border rule provides: the ability to settle expectations regarding the exclusion of others, as if it were "a legitimate and natural baseline." There's nothing natural about it, but such is the long shadow of epistemic individualism, which grounds the Western philosophical tradition. As philosopher Judith Butler has noted, the nation-state stands in for Western thought's central figure, the white, propertied man requiring violent "self-defense" in an imagined Hobbesian war of all against all. A phantasmagorical threat is posited, against whom violence is justified, in the name of "security" for those considered to belong to the state, to possess the correct property of selfhood. Questions of citizenship cannot be unmoored from histories racialized status property; Black people were denied citizenship because they were owned.

The eighteenth-century philosopher Jeremy Bentham wrote that "property is nothing but a basis of expectation," the "established expectation" of being able to "derive such and such advantage from the thing possessed." Property, constituted in the continued and assured fulfilment of an expectation, can be wholly relative, and stripped bare, until all that's left is the established expectation that others will be excluded. Border rule is thus a method of propertization—the processes by which a thing takes on the form of modern property—not in the sense that it bestows citizens today with material property or the collective resources to flourish but that it maintains a status property, bestowing real advantages presumed to be derivable by only some because others are excluded from that status. Calls to secure the border project a desire for the exclusion of others to be a constantly settled expectation, with the certainty of individual property rights in the Western tradition.

It is a strange sort of ownership that inheres in making certain the fact of others' exclusion. Especially exclusion from an institution (the nation-state) that the citizen "owner" does not materially possess. Were exclusion not so axiomatic to deeply entrenched understandings of property rights, such an empty property status would make little sense as a thing to desire. But as things are, border regimes uphold what philosopher Eva von Redecker calls "phantom possession." This is the form these expectations of exclusion take—a violently protected entitlement, where other forms of racialized and gendered dominion over other human beings and nonhuman life once stood under law, in the forms of slavery and coverture.

In the absence of legal titles of ownership that once existed, phantom possession is compensation in the form of continued white supremacist domination through structural advantages, laws, norms, and expectations. "After abolition," von Redecker writes, "new institutional arrangements can assume the functions of stabilizing phantom possession," including "border regimes, detention centers, prisons, and abortion bans."

For the phantom owner, described by von Redecker as "in desperate need of restoring their domains of sovereignty," border rule offers the assurance of racialized exclusion and removal. "I voted for this!" the MAGA loyalists can post gleefully under ICE raid videos. It is a spectral dominion, often delivered in the form of a twisted reality-TV-style spectacle. And it is for this reason that the hardened border can also hold such strong appeal as phantom property even for nonwhite citizens excluded from all other sites of value accumulation and ownership. Von Redecker's key claim, though, is that authoritarian accumulations of phantom possession are not "liberalism's nemesis" but "a contradiction that liberalism itself bore to the world" by tying freedom to the modern form of property. We see this not only in white nationalist ressentiment but also in the certainty with which liberals today speak of the exclusion of migrants as some obviously justifiable aspect of nation-statehood. "Just the reality of being a nation."

Like phantom pain in a lost limb, the feeling of phantom ownership is real and based in real experience. The metaphor has limits, though. A person who has lost an arm but continues to insist, "I know I have two hands" would likely be treated as experiencing a delusion; if they tried to act with the certainty of having two hands (say, without the help of a prosthetic limb), attempting to open doors or catch keys with a phantom limb, they would continuously hit against the physical fact of their arm's absence. Such a person might well need support coming to terms with this new reality, but nothing in their material surroundings and social interactions would provide grounds for the continued conviction that the lost arm remained firmly in place. The phantom possessions of vengeful nationalist backlash work quite differently: a world conspires to help uphold such supremacist delusions as real. Border rule pumps blood into phantom limbs. The property relation, in terms of the "basis of expectation" for continuing to derive "certain advantages," is far more than an apparition.

"Expectation as property is not only overdetermined by differential racialization and dispossession," writes scholar of US settler colonialism Alyosha Goldstein, "but acquires capacity through specific presumptions of entitlement and certainty produced in law."

Goldstein is addressing how, throughout the history of the US, expectations of white entitlement have been solidified into certainties through laws and policies of racialized propertization. Indigenous slaughter and dispossession, westward expansion and the promise to settlers of "individual liberty" through land ownership, "the rescinded promise of land redistribution for formerly enslaved African Americans during Reconstruction," and the use of public domain for the extraction of natural resources, among other interventions, all produce and reinforce expectations of entitlement as world-ordering certainties.

Settler colonial states offer particularly striking examples of how expectations of dominion can become settled into epistemic certainties of entitlement, even on brazenly stolen land. The anthropologist Eva Mackey calls this "settler certainty." According to Mackey:

> This certainty emerges from a set of stories that are grounded in delusions of entitlement, which are based on irrational and

> illogical arguments that should make sense to no one, not even those who created them and turned them into laws. They are socially embedded, unconscious expectations of how the world will work to reaffirm social locations, perceptions, and benefits of privilege that have been legitimated through repeated experiences across lifetimes and generations.

In *The Age of Insecurity*, Astra Taylor also draws attention to the explicit weaponization of uncertainty by the Canadian government and private sector in response to the success of (hard-won) victories in court to see Indigenous land titles recognized. She highlights the case of *Delgamuukw v. British Columbia*, launched by the Gitxsan and Wet'suwet'en Nations in 1984.

"As oral cultures, the Gitxsan and Wet'suwet'en Nations did not document land ownership through written contracts and deeds, and the plaintiffs set a precedent by using oral traditions, rather than written documentation, as legal proof," Taylor notes. "They affirmed their possession of the land through the Gitxsan adaawk and Wet'suwet'en kungax, verbal collections of legends, laws, rituals, and traditions Elders presented as evidence, much to the judge's consternation." Settler certainty, that is, discounted as illegible those forms of proof outside the language game of colonial documentation. And thus indigenous proof was invisibilized in court. One judge scoffed at "witnesses singing songs" and ruled against the Gitxsan and Wet'suwet'en peoples. Eventually, though, Canada's Supreme Court ruled in 1997 to recognize the principle of Aboriginal title as a form of collective ownership (but did not rule on any specific land in question). As Taylor reports:

> The verdict caused the private sector to panic . . . In emails and faxes, corporate lobbyists urged government officials to push

> First Nations to surrender their newly expanded rights to ensure the "certainty" of commercial interests . . . A "certainty working group" meeting was arranged by the BC [British Columbia] Treaty Negotiations advisory committee lawyer, who counselled that a treaty process should seek "an end of Aboriginal rights and title"—an approach the United Nations has strongly opposed.
>
> Despite the Canadian Supreme Court's recognition of Aboriginal title and the support of international human rights law, the fight for Indigenous sovereignty remains profoundly lopsided, with impoverished communities going up against multinational behemoths, their powerful provincial lobbyists, and the government agencies that abet them.

These are the very activities of settler certainty that Mackey also highlights—the panicked concerns over losing profits as settler landowners, yes, but something deeper than that. The reaction is one of furious disorientation and inability to accept that something as certain, as bedrock, as settled property relations could be challenged.

Mackey focuses on the US and Canada as her case studies, but her analysis applies just as aptly to Israeli settler certainty and the indignance with which Zionists react when it is questioned. We need only consider the genocide in Gaza to appreciate the extraordinary danger of fantasies of certainty when it comes to settler entitlement. Nationhood mythologies, unbounded gunpower, Western property logics, apartheid policies, hideous racism and religious chauvinism, imperial interests, historic trauma, and necropolitical colonial administration combine to posit—absurdly—that a seventy-eight-year-old settler nation-state, based on a one-hundred-fifty-year-old political ideology, is somehow inherently, transhistorically, and eternally justified as the dominion of a manufactured Jewish majority.

"The precarious and illogical claims to settler sovereignty must be constantly reinvented and defended," Mackey writes, because claims to land and ways of being that unsettle the dominant property form "reveal settler certainties as fantasies of entitlement" that are upheld and affirmed but ultimately illegitimate. As theorist Robert Nichols has put it, "Indigenous modes of relating to the land will not fit easily within either private or collective property systems because they will not simply rehearse the drama that has already unfolded in Western, European contexts."

Goldstein also highlights that settler certainty requires "disavowal" and "willful ignorance" on behalf of the settler—their settled expectations of entitlement must be imagined as justified and natural (hence the certainty), not as an advantage maintained through force and the threat of it. For the open ethno-supremacist, the fantasy is one of inherent racial and cultural superiority. For the liberal capitalist defender of ethnostates and other racist border regimes, willful ignorance takes the form of upholding these property and citizenship systems and imagining they are not racial regimes, but simply rules-based and reasoned forms of territorial sovereignty.

My focus here has been limited to settler colonial states; however, the doubling down on anti-immigrant border rule has been just as pronounced in the UK and parts of Western Europe. In these cases we might use the term colonial certainty, rather than settler certainty, to describe the settled expectations of entitlement wherein immigration laws, enforcement, and discourses work to settle expectations around nation-state belonging and (phantom) possession shaped by global racial empire. Borders continue to ground colonial expectations around who can move or remain freely in each nation-state and who can be dispossessed, displaced or detained. When liberals treat "securing" the border as somehow obviously justified, they shore up this colonial certainty, willfully ignoring the entanglements of colonization, racialization and property.

Mackey does not use "certainty" in an explicitly Wittgensteinian sense, but I'd argue that we should understand settler/colonial certainty in this way, insofar as it is a frame of expectation held fast by those inculcated into it. Colonial certainty is a world-ordering hinge on which countless other practices turn, resistant to doubt and challenge, giving shape to what is deemed credible and legible, but—crucially—without deeper justification.

Who could deem the maintenance of this racialized phantom possession, colonial certainty, justified? Sure, an ethnonationalist who believes in the exclusive blood-and-soil right of a certain racial or ethnic group to dominion over a specific territory. This is, I would hope, a justification that the rest of us reject. Yet this is precisely the ghoulish property relation upheld by liberal defenses of border security.

Liberal politicians who affirm the incontestability of border rule and the necessity of migrant exclusion (framed as security) might imagine themselves merely upholding orderly governance around accessing a given legal status in a country; what they do, though, is ratify settled expectations around an historic-racial schema when it comes to the border as a demarcator of (phantom) property.

When the historian Hont took "crisis-mongers" to task in the early nineties, it was to challenge what he observed as paranoiac concern over the supposed crisis of the nation-state under globalization. The nation-state was not, Hont argued, facing some new, terminal crisis but was an assemblage inherently riddled by "permanent crisis," which, if we recall, Hont advised we just call "normality." Hont noted, citing thinkers including Immanuel Kant and Adam Smith, that since the formation of the sovereign nation-state, anxieties have arisen about its viability in a world of global trade and imperial competition, as well as extreme inequalities and competing interests and tensions within territories. Has it, Hont asked, "ever been possible to justify the existence of 'nation-states' as sovereign occupiers of certain definite tracts of the surface of the globe"?

Hont perceived a problem of *justification* attending the story of the nation-state, relating to the property logics on which it relies. Or rather an imagined problem of justification. The purported crisis for the nation-state under globalization, argued Hont, was no more than the latest iteration of structural tensions inherent to the nation-state. As he put it:

> Adam Smith, for example, could not be easily mistaken to have been an opponent of modern economic regimes based on private property. But he nonetheless wisely explained to his students at the University of Glasgow in the 1760s that private property could never be justified to the degree to which one's right to life and personal bodily security could be. But if the legitimation of private property remains contentious, national group property is even more so as we still do not possess a theory that can provide an ultimate justification for it.

WITH THE term "national group property," Hont is not here invoking the racialized (phantom) property status I explored above, but his broader point stands: a certain property logic can be used to justify border regimes, but it is not itself justified.

Scholars like philosopher Daniel Loick have done important recent work showing how purported justifications for the institution of property consistently fail; it is beyond my purview to repeat those arguments here. Suffice it for our purposes to emphasize that border logic relies on exclusionary modern property logic. And the inability to justify border rule outside of the racialized expectations of the property form should trouble the self-avowedly nonracist liberals who call for "secure" borders. But this would give too much credit, both to liberals and to the place of justification in all of our actions. Without deeper grounds, without justification, a structure can *seem* fragile, which partly explains paranoiac drives to secure an already entrenched institution, and the readiness to invoke a story of crisis; but so long as the vast array of bordering activities continues, the absence of justifications is—alas—no real risk to the border regime.

We like to imagine that our actions are, for the most part, justified. But this overestimates how often we really engage in activities of justification. The search for justification mostly attends to already existing practices and institutions, which started and continue with or without such justification, and will persist or crumble for reasons that likely have little to do with whether or not broad agreement is reached about justifications for the practices in question.

This doesn't render a desire for justifications useless or a bad thing. It can be extremely useful to point out that a common practice or institution that purports to be legitimate is without justification. Or to draw attention to where the language game of justification comes to an end in various contexts. This illuminates the shape of our certainties. Wittgenstein put it this way in his *Philosophical Investigations*:

> If I have exhausted the justifications I have reached bedrock, and my spade is turned. Then I am inclined to say: "This is simply what I do."

For a vast number of our common behaviors, if we are asked, "But why do you do that?" our ability to give reasons comes to an end at a certain point. (Consider the "but why?" conversation with a child.) Practices and conventions are embedded in collective "forms of life"—inculcated behaviors and inherited world-pictures. "I did not get my picture of the world by satisfying myself of its correctness; nor do I have it because I am satisfied of its correctness," Wittgenstein wrote in his later notes. "No: it is the inherited background against which I distinguish between true and false." We learn to judge *within* systems of judgment that we inherit.

This might sound a bit like brainwashing, but it's more basic than that; it's simply how we learn to make meaning and communicate and function in the world. Most of the time, the system of judgment stays in the background, like water to fish, and it would make no sense to ask whether it is justified or not. But sometimes we are compelled to do so.

The Democratic Party advisor Cecilia Muñoz exemplified this when she said that "removing folks who don't qualify under the law" is "just the reality of being a nation." Questions can be asked about whether *a given person* gets to qualify and what counts as "qualify[ing] under law"; questions could also be asked about the *specifics of those laws* (immigration laws do change, after all); questions could also be asked about the history of those laws and rules. But when it comes to justifying the system of nation-state inclusion and exclusion as a whole, the "inherited background," justification is exhausted—these propertized divisions are "simply" or "just" what we do.

But we simply must do otherwise. There are currently an estimated 123 million displaced people worldwide. We do not need to accept the exclusionary nation-state as a given.

We have reached bedrock when it comes to the colonial certainty of border rule; it is not justified, yet property-as-border logic grounds various and violent bordering activities, which in turn hold the expectations and delusions of border rule firmly in place as certainties. It is impossibly circular, but no more so than so many of the institutions and norms that continue without deeper justification, as simply what we do or what is done to us. Which is why the question of *doing otherwise* is crucial. If, again, "what stands fast does so not because it is intrinsically obvious or convincing" but because it "is rather held fast by what lies around it," we must displace what lies around the border, as an arrangement, holding the border in place as a certainty. This is the work of denaturalizing settled expectations, and disrupting the activities that keep them settled.

SCHOLAR-ACTIVISTS like Walia have put forward powerful arguments for a politics of not just open borders but of no nation-state borders. "Empires crumble," she writes, "capitalism is not inevitable, gender is not biology, whiteness is not immutable, prisons are not inescapable, and borders are not natural law." No one pretends we can easily envision a borderless world from our current vantage point, which holds the bordered nation-state as the sine qua non of global politics. The idea that exclusionary, bordered states constitute the only feasible world-ordering system does not follow in turn. The philosopher Wendy Brown has argued, for example, that while democracies must be somehow bounded—if "we" are to rule as the people, we must have a constitutive sense of who and what that "we" will be—this "we" need not be constituted by the brutal demarcations of nationality and property logics. It is historically myopic, not to mention an act of Indigenous erasure, to insist that a demos must be demarcated by a logic of propertization, exclusion and scarcity rather than by a recognition of our mutual, planetary interdependence.

We can take inspiration from existing challenges to colonial certainty and border rule: the revolutionary struggle and governance models of the Zapatistas, the autonomous administration of Rojava in Syria, or the Indigenous land actions and climate struggles against neocolonial rule and capitalist extraction around the world. These radical interventions, rare and embattled as they might be, model critical practices for liberation that can come into the realm of possibility.

I would be lying if I said that I could imagine, really imagine, a borderless world, even as nation-state border regimes again and again show their violence and unsuitability for collective survival on a heating planet. This is perhaps a problem of my imagination, but if so, it's a shared problem in a shared "inherited background." A world without borders, or even a world with extremely porous borders, would be a world without the specific set of certainties that ground modern political intelligibility. "If the ability to act always relies on existing patterns of action, it seems unclear how anything new . . . could ever be possible," the philosopher von Redecker notes, also invoking Wittgenstein's bedrock metaphor to describe the "the structures that themselves create the tracks on which other actions take place" such that existing practices become "regarded as being entirely without alternative."

It feels impossible to imagine worlds otherwise because it becomes impossible to conceptually develop them through lived practices, to shift the riverbed of thoughts through activities that disturb the river's sediment. It's not like we can just dabble in borderlessness or experiment with open borders in the face of a brutal border regime (such experiments are the preserve of billionaires). As is the case with prison abolition, I also don't know any border abolitionist who ignores the importance of exigent struggles for better state policies simply because they think the state shouldn't exist as it does—and this is a good thing. Immediate action against the worst excesses of far-right nationalism is crucial. It is also consistent with longer-term efforts to denaturalize the colonial certainties of border rule. The bedrock of border rule may bend our spades when we hit against it, but as von Redecker also reminds us, "few structures are so petrified that there is no possible subcontext in which they could be suspended."

"If the construction of and defence of certainty is at the core of coloniality, then settler uncertainty may actually be necessary for decolonization," writes Mackey. What would it look like to unsettle, rather than affirm, the conviction that there is something natural, obvious, and reasonable about the settled expectations of border exclusion? If border rule is the consistently settled expectation of (racialized) exclusion, what does it mean to thwart such an expectation? Exposing and challenging border logic is only a start; it should give a few liberals pause to realize the groundlessness of their believing. But it is the activities of border rule that produce and sustain hardened borders as axiomatic; unless those activities and behaviors are disrupted, the fact of exclusionary borders will not change.

There are examples to build upon and learn from. When protesters swarmed New York's John F. Kennedy International Airport in 2017 to counter Trump's first Muslim ban and cab drivers refused to drop passengers there; when the immigrant rebels of the gilets noirs in France occupied a terminal at Charles de Gaulle Airport in Paris, in direct resistance to Air France's role as "the official deporter of the French state"; when Minneapolis rose up against ICE agents who stormed the city in early 2026, and rapid response networks, militant activists, organized labor, and communities fought back with historic mass strikes, boycotts, blockades, and countless acts of mutual aid. When people lock their doors to ICE and hide their immigrant neighbors, continuing the legacy of the 1980s sanctuary movement. When people make the identities of these agents of terror public, unsettling expectations of anonymous impunity.

Willem van Spronsen, a sixty-nine-year-old activist, was shot dead in 2019 by police when he attempted to incinerate a fleet of empty ICE vans outside an immigration detention center in Tacoma, Washington. He wrote in a short manifesto, "I have an unshakable abhorrence for injustice. That is what brings me here." He acted with certainty. An ICE representative at the time of Van Spronsen's death stated, misleadingly, "This could have resulted in the mass murder of staff and detainees housed at the facility." Van Spronsen did not target any buildings holding immigrants or ICE staff. It's true that he was armed with a home-assembled AR-15, and we do not know whether he exchanged gunfire with the four Tacoma police officers who arrived on the scene; none of them were injured.

Van Spronsen's solitary yet absolute rebellion understood how the techniques of fascist terror presuppose quotidian infrastructure. Border enforcement uses the same streets, the same highways, the same airports as the rest of us. Van Spronsen went for the vans. "You don't have to burn the motherfucker down, but are you going to just stand by?" he wrote. None of us, through individual acts, can burn the motherfucker down. Obstruction can take many forms, but only collective, aligned, and continuously practiced actions on scales large and small, against the gears of the necropolitical deportation machine, could render individual extreme actions like Van Spronsen's unnecessary, and the activities of border rule less certain.

The work to stop ICE and other extremist articulations of

authoritarian border regimes could not be more urgent. But our orientation cannot be limited to containing the excesses of border policing. Without unsettling the property form and the logics on which border rule stands, the violence of exclusionary dominium will continue to stand and give rise to these sorts of fascist formations. This property critique of the border encompasses calls to abolish ICE, calls emerging from within a broader abolitionist framework and bringing together Black liberation, anticolonial, anticapitalist and immigrant rights struggles. What would it mean to unsettle, to make uncertain, the expectations of (racialized) exclusion that undergird the property form? What would it mean to render Cecilia Muñoz's statement, with which we started this chapter, anything but obvious?

Indigenous land claims mentioned above offer examples of challenges to settler certainty. They are not the only interventions in the presumed property order from which to draw inspiration. In her book *In Defense of Looting*, Vicky Osterweil points to looting, that is, "a crowd of people publicly, openly, and directly taking things in the midst of riot and social unrest," as a "method of direct redistribution of wealth" and a challenge to the property regime:

> Though no single instance of looting is on its own sufficient to transform society, obviously, looting—at least when carried out by Black, poor, or Indigenous people—will always be strenuously and vigorously disavowed by the powers that be because it points to and immediately enacts a different relationship to property, a different history.

It's notable, as Osterweil highlights, that the "specter of slaves freeing themselves is American history's first image of black looters." The fervid overreaction to instances of looting during protest movements points to a certainty unsettled.

In a similar vein, von Redecker points to the "precious period of two weeks" in 2020 when a 136-room Sheraton hotel in Minneapolis was taken over by activists, including hotel workers, "with a certain level of consent by the former management," and turned into a temporary home for unhoused people and others who needed shelter in the midst of the George Floyd uprisings. Some dubbed it the "Share-a-ton." Decentralized volunteers provided food, medicine, and other necessities. Handwritten signs with the word "sanctuary" were posted on the windows. An experiment within a long tradition of nonaccumulative processes that have challenged the propertization of everyday life: stealing away, squatting, looting, redistributing, sheltering, building sanctuary.

"This sanctuary, a place hardly intelligible in the existing order of things, is one example for what is meant by interstices," von Redecker notes of the Share-a-ton, describing an interstice as "a short-lived anomaly" which nonetheless "forms a crack through which a possible different future illuminates the present." She adds, "The Share-a-ton did not last, facing eviction as well as internal collapse, which goes to show that revolution in one interstice is impossible. What is needed is more of those breaks with the same."

3

Cis Certainty, Trans Knowledge

> *When we say: "Every word in language signifies something" we have so far said* nothing whatever*; unless we have explained exactly what distinction we wish to make.*
>
> Ludwig Wittgenstein, *Philosophical Investigations*

DURING THE confirmation hearings of US Supreme Court Justice Ketanji Brown Jackson, Republican Senator Marsha Blackburn attempted to deliver a well-worn gotcha, beloved of anti-trans activists. "Can you provide a definition of the word 'woman'?" the conservative senator asked the liberal justice.

"Can I provide a definition? No, I can't," responded Jackson. Had the judge finished there, her answer would have been perfect. No one can provide a definition— a necessary and sufficient definition to cover all cases and only those cases to which the word "woman" is correctly applied. This is not because there's something strange and definition-defying about the word "woman" in particular. Rather, definitions rarely do the work that we might imagine they do in language. Jackson should have simply rejected the question, but, no doubt flustered by hours of racist haranguing from Republican inquisitors, she added, "I'm not a biologist."

Blackburn, who has spent a career decimating women's bodily autonomy, spat back: "The fact that you can't give me a straight answer about something as fundamental as what a woman is underscores the dangers of the kind of progressive education that we are hearing about." The right-wing media and commentariat—Blackburn's intended audience—duly followed suit with aghast headlines and tweets, appalled that a nominated Supreme Court Justice could not, or would not, answer this "simple" question.

In their readiness to lambast the first Black woman nominated to the Supreme Court, and to take any chance to spew anti-trans vitriol, the reactionary response appeared to miss that, in a significant way, Jackson had given a conservative answer. The suggestion that it is only biologists who can and should determine the definition of the word "woman" gets dangerously close to suggesting that gender *is* biology. This is shorthand for the claim that the reductive taxonomies of high school–level science should supervene on all realities of sexed and gendered existence—the core of many anti-trans claims.

In deferring to biologists as rightful arbiters on the matter, Jackson's claim was somewhat more careful: after all, it is biologists who largely reject that dimorphic sex characteristics determine a person's gender, or that biological sex is as rigidly fixed and dyadic as transphobes insist. It's no accident that far-right lawmakers can rely on only a few fringe doctors to uphold a gender- and sex-essentialist line when attempting to ban transition-related healthcare for kids and adults.

The problem with Jackson's response is two-fold: Firstly, the meaning of "woman" should not be left to only a specific type of expert. Biologists don't have some special access to the concept "woman." Meanwhile, countless historic harms have been produced by upholding the medical establishment as gatekeepers of sex and gender assignment. Secondly, Jackson was wrong to even entertain that such a definition of the word "woman" is available in the first place. This is not how the world works, and this is not how language works.

In response to the "define woman!" demand, I have long turned to Wittgenstein's thoughts on meaning. To those who obsess over mythically fixed and absolute definitions, I've emphasized Wittgenstein's reminder that "the meaning of a word is its use in the language": that the meanings of terms are not bound by strict, preexisting rules; "correct" usage is determined collectively. This can work in our favor; this can work against it, too. But what this is *not* is some trivial point about assigning signs and symbols to people and things. For the ways we make meaning together undergird our world-making possibilities. Nor is this a question of showing liberal deference to personal identity, limited to visibility and representation. It's about who is and is not permitted to produce and reproduce the world as they see fit, who is subjected to suspicion and doubt, and which forms of gendered life are accorded the presumptions of certainty.

My interest here is not to argue with the far right. The right plays a cynical game; any tactic will do if it serves to uphold strict gender conformity and the denial of bodily autonomy. Their investment lies not in correctly defining "woman" to support women but in ordering lives in accordance with the heteropatriarchal nuclear family and the maintenance of white standing and private property.

And it is revealing that the right's supposedly natural ontology of binary gender takes such extraordinary authoritarian work to try to enforce. From banning trans children from sports teams, bathrooms, and access to healthcare to—as did one Florida school board—mandating all children, including cis children, get parental permission to use a nickname, as a blanket way to prevent trans kids from being called their own names in school. After all, a regime of gender conformity requires broad social control.

The point being: the far right doesn't care if its claims are groundless and its arguments invalid. And they will not wait to see whether all aspects of their bans and criminalization plans stand up in federal court before enacting them. The right makes laws into realities through violence and violent realities through law. Proving them incoherent and incorrect is hardly a bulwark.

This is also true of the protests and campaigns of the transphobic liberals and trans-exclusionary feminists—professional philosophers and prominent writers like philosopher Kathleen Stock and journalist Hadley Freeman among numerous others—who use alleged reason and reasonableness as their cudgel, and fiercely bordered womanhood as their concern. There is usefulness, however, in clarifying the glaring poverty of their thinking, given the huge platforms they're accorded by the *Guardian*, the *New York Times*, the BBC, and many more vaunted establishments.

Despite what these figures insist upon, our language games—our activities of making sense—lend themselves most readily to practices of trans affirmation. Numerous brilliant transfeminist scholars and scientists, among others, have shown the intellectual flaws and patriarchal, not to mention racist, underpinnings of gender essentialist positions. I hope only to add to their efforts. I write to appreciate the necessarily collective and difficult nature of meaning making, which is to write not only against the right and its anti-trans bedfellows but *for* something: for an expansive feminism grounded in shared knowledge and liberatory uncertainties rather than oppressive doubts and entrenched certainties.

Anti-trans activists imagine their insistence on sex-gender binarism as a conclusion drawn from well-grounded knowledge. They have confused that which they hold certain with that which they can claim to know—I say this as an almost logical point. If, as Wittgenstein reminds us, we can only know what we can possibly and sensibly doubt, and ideologues of cisness assert that sex cannot be doubted, then it is not the sort of thing that they can talk of knowing either. Cis certainty forecloses knowledge of sex and gender—categories that arise in a multitude of language games and shared forms of life. This ignorance becomes clear when anti-trans crusaders insist that they know the real definition of "woman."

WHAT DO I mean when I say that Justice Brown Jackson was right that she could not give a definition of women? Something like what Wittgenstein suggests in his *Philosophical Investigations* when he notes, "Remember that we sometimes demand definitions for the sake not of their content, but of their form. Our requirement is an architectural one; the definition a kind of ornamental coping that supports nothing." It is indeed, to borrow from trollish online parlance, a cope. "Define!" the anti-trans campaigners cry, clinging desperately to an austere world-picture against which the abundance of gender variance, desire, and need continues to push. The call to define "woman" is a demand for a sharp closure to a term that, like most every term, has none; this is the form of definition on which trans eliminationists insist. But it does not, when challenged, support trans-exclusionary conclusions.

The mistake is to think that we need knowledge of a word's determinate definition to correctly use it, when it is existing practices of usage that definitions attempt to capture post hoc. When the use of a word changes, definitions are updated; dictionaries are updated to align with general use, not vice versa. This is not a teleological process—dictionary definitions don't evolve toward some endpoint. We use words, we communicate; definitions are limited but sometimes useful snapshots of these practices. Does this mean there is no such thing as incorrect language use? Of course not, but we'll get to that.

Given its weakness, I've long been surprised by the fierce appeal of the "Define woman!" game to so-called gender skeptics (a misnomer if I've ever heard one, consumed as they are by their notions of gender). Helen Joyce, an editor at the *Economist*, author and prolific purveyor of anti-trans talking points, wrote, "There's a circularity to the mantra that trans women are women, which raises and leaves unanswered the question of what then the word woman means." Matt Walsh, a far-right political commentator, brought out an online documentary in 2022 titled *What Is a Woman?* in which he engages in faux-naive interviews with trans people, gender studies theorists, physicians, and mental health professionals who provide gender-affirming care. When asked to define the word "woman," the interviewees' answers are often lengthy, complex, thoughtful and, yes, indeterminate: they resist and reject the idea that there is one simple way to define what a woman is. Yet the refusal to give a one-sentence definition is treated as an intellectual failure by Walsh—a proof of "woke" delusion and distance from reality.

In turn, I would like to ask a definition enthusiast like Walsh to give me a definition of the word "game"—an example made famous in the *Philosophical Investigations*.

So, what is a game? No doubt you can give me a wealth of examples: chess, Scrabble, tennis, Fortnite, Sim City, craps. What defines these things as games? The most obvious answer is that you play them. But that's not a definitional answer. A game is not simply "that which you play"; otherwise, a musical instrument would also fall under the category "game." "A complete episode or period of play, ending in a definite result," suggests the dictionary—but we don't call, say, piano competitions games, and we do sometimes use the word "game" for certain practices that don't have an end—and this does not confuse people.

Is a game definitionally something you play *with* others? That's not quite right: numerous card games and computer games are played solo. Is a game something that can be won or lost? No, there are ties, and there are noncompetitive games—games of dress-up and make believe. Some games involve groups, some balls, some boards or fields; some are played professionally, most are amateur. We could keep grabbing for a definition, but any single one will come up short: there is no one definition of the word "game" that I could give you now, or that you could give me, that will sufficiently, uniquely and correctly cover each and every example of things in the world we call, or might in future call, games. Which is to say: there's no one final definition of the word "game."

It's an ancient philosophical lampoon: To Plato's definition of a man as an "animal, bipedal and featherless," Diogenes plucked a chicken and declared, "Here is Plato's man." The joke only works because we already know how to use the term "man" correctly, and we don't apply it to naked chickens. Our facility with the term has nothing to do with our having some strange access to a hidden transcendental essence belonging to each categorized thing. "When philosophers use a word," Wittgenstein notes, "and try to grasp the *essence* of the thing, one must always ask oneself: is the word ever actually used in this way in the language-game which is its original home?"

There is no one definition of the word "game," but that's not a failure of the concept or our ability to use it. We can and do speak meaningfully of games all the time. And this isn't only a point about the word "game" but about the array of games—practices—we tend to call language. But let's take one step, or move, at a time: let's start with the term "game." (Readers who know their Wittgenstein, feel free to jump ahead a few paragraphs.)

The things we call "games" don't share a single determining definition, because "game" is what Wittgenstein calls a "family resemblance" concept. There is no one essential common feature that all things we call "game" share; rather we see, as he puts it, "a complicated network of similarities overlapping and crisscrossing." Like resemblance in a family: tennis has in common with football that balls are involved, but not the use of rackets; football has in common with field hockey (but not tennis) that each team has eleven players on a pitch; these are team games, and so is Dungeons and Dragons, in which there are no balls, but there is a board, as with chess. And so this web of that which we call "game" stretches out, like an interconnected but technically unbounded set of Venn Diagrams.

"For how is the concept of a game bounded?" Wittgenstein asked, "What still counts as a game and what no longer does? Can you give the boundary? No. You can draw one; for none has so far been drawn. (But that never troubled you before when you used the word 'game.')" It does not trouble use and meaning making that no one thing or essence underlies every single example of a concept or term—be it game, number, woman, man. As Wittgenstein notes, "We extend our concept of number"—but this could be any concept—"as in spinning a thread we twist fiber on fiber. And the strength of the thread does not reside in the fact that some one fiber runs through its whole length, but in the overlapping of many fibers."

I'm talking about games here, as Wittgenstein did, because it's a way to illustrate a broader point about terms, concepts and constructs, how they carry meaning and where their boundaries lie. A vast number of terms, which we readily use all the time—most terms, I'd say—constitute "family resemblance" concepts. Concepts are unbounded, and we draw their boundaries as we collectively use them, and as we use them for different purposes and in different contexts (in different language games). The world is not divided up according to predetermined categories, sharp objects and ordered things, to which we attach words. Want to know the meaning of a word? Observe how it's used. Observe, too, how meanings can change.

Transphobes claim that trans-inclusive meanings—the inclusion of trans women in our meaning of "woman"—are signs of some linguistic free-for-all. That without a clear, fixed definition, just about anyone, including a cis man, can simply label themselves "woman" and with no more than that utterance, expect to be recognized as such. Such hypotheticals have little bearing on what happens in the world. It's just not the case that one declarative speech act, "I am a woman," serves as an induction into the category "woman," because meaning making and understanding are not just practices of naming. Paranoiac claims that supporting trans rights will lead to a spate of predatory men pretending to be women to access women's spaces are worse than specious. They purposefully ignore that it is trans people who are constantly exposed to violence for simply existing in public spaces: In a 2020 British Gallop poll, 80 percent of trans respondents reported that they had suffered from transphobic hate crimes.

What a half-witted understanding of how language works, to think that we find ourselves in semantic chaos, that "woman" can mean anything, simply because the concept is not delimited by a reductive definition. Patently, we do not lose the ability to speak meaningfully of women. First and foremost, because you can't change a word's meaning alone. If you, as an individual, decide to use a word to mean something it doesn't currently mean, people around you will assume you don't know how to correctly use the word. If you one day decide to say "cake" instead of "door," and you ask someone to "open the cake" when you want to say "open the door," your request will fail to get the door opened; and you'll have to say, "Oh, by cake, I mean door"—you will need to translate into the shared background language in order to communicate, and thus fail to create new meaning. Meaning isn't and can't be some totally subjective or relative thing, just because it isn't immutably fixed. Rather, think of it in materialist terms: historically situated and reliant on certain processes, practices and interactions and embedded in forms of life.

As feminist philosopher Isabel G. Gamero Cabrera notes, using this Wittgensteinian point against anti-trans claims of arbitrary gendered term use, "Nobody can entirely change the use of an already existing word or give to it a completely new meaning, without taking into account previous uses and the practices linked to this word, that is, its grammar . . . [Transphobes] imagine a hypothetical and unrealistic situation in which someone arbitrarily and individually changes his/her sex."

What is realistic? What actually happens? That trans women, living as they choose, *make sense* within the category "woman," within the meaning of the word, when the word "woman" is rightly understood as unclosed but no less material, no less real, for that fact.

I grant that we leave too much hanging unaddressed in simply pointing out that "woman" rightly applies to trans women because we use it accordingly and it works. There are some valid questions about categorization to consider. Also using Wittgenstein to argue against transphobic essentialist demands, philosopher Cressida Heyes has fairly recognized our need to respond to the concern that "if you are a feminist, then you need to make generalizations about women, for this is the essence of feminist politics!"

Do we forgo the possibility of speaking as women and for women if we refuse the idea that there is something essential about womanhood that delineates it? Surely, no more than we lose the ability to speak meaningfully of games simply because we can't clarify in advance where the boundaries of the concept lie. It's a beautiful thing, or at least could be, that we can't make sense alone! We do draw boundaries as we go; where they are drawn is not a question of fealty to a concept's mythical essence, but how we live with and through and against the world as we've found it, collectively. The content of "woman," what we mean when we say it, or when we identify as woman, for those of us who do, is indeed a matter of overlapping threads, made stronger for the fact that not one piece of thread must run through the whole rope.

Heyes's Wittgensteinian point here is clarifying:

> Let us consider the construct that we call "women." I don't just mean white, middle-class, heterosexual, able-bodied, young, attractive, western women, but all women. What is common to them all? Don't say: "there must be something in common or they wouldn't be called 'women.' " Likewise, don't say: "If women have nothing in common, then how can feminism form a political movement?" Look and see what the construct of women consists of, and what women might have

> in common. For, if you look, you will not see something that is common to all, but similarities, relationships, and a whole series of them at that.

The insistence that there is a singular "women's experience," exclusive to women assigned female at birth, is empirically false. It doesn't exist; try to locate and name it, and, I assure you, you will end up playing the same unsatisfying game that we played above with the term "game." My trans women comrades who transitioned in adulthood may not have shared my experience growing up female, but nor do I have any idea what it feels like to grow up female in, say occupied Palestine or rural Arkansas —the fact of sharing female assignment at birth hardly closes such experiential gaps produced by stratifications of race, class, disability and all manner of lived differences. Rather, as trans theorist and author Grace Lavery has noted, "Reality—the reality shared by women, actual women, in the world—really does matter for feminism. Metaphysical definitions of the category 'woman' really, really don't."

We recognize a concept through its "similarities, relationships, and a whole series of them at that"—overlapping, nonidentical, the fibers of a thread—this isn't a normative claim, but simply the nature of a family resemblance concept. Those of us interested in robust, transnational, antiracist and antifascist feminisms can be pleased that "woman" is such a construct. Trans-exclusionary feminism, meanwhile, seeks something more threadbare.

When transphobes like J. K. Rowling invoke the experience that supposedly all and only cis women share, they delimit the women's experiences that get to count; actual living women are erased, and more often than not, white women get to stand for all women. The universalization of gender binarism is inextricable from five hundred years of global racial empire, demonizing and eradicating gender variance when encountered in colonized peoples, and enforcing racial hierarchies through the exclusion of Black people and other people of color from the Western Enlightenment's gendered schema.

The dominant system of gender binarism was imposed upon the rest of the world through the process of European colonization. The combination of exported Christianity and Enlightenment scientism produced specific hierarchies of racialization and gender/sex in service of empire. This is what feminist philosopher Maria Lugones calls the "coloniality of gender"—the "dehumanization of colonized and African-diasporic women as lacking gender, one of the marks of the [Western Enlightenment conception of] human, and thus being reduced to labor and to raw sex, conceived as non-socializable sexual difference—their offspring also slaves from birth and thus not their own."

Those who fiercely attempt to guard the category of woman in the name of feminism only echo the white suffragists who drew a line around white women as the subject of their feminist politics and vehemently excluded Black women from their fight for voting rights. The 19th Amendment, ratified on August 18, 1920, is often celebrated for granting US women the right to vote—a fact that quite literally removes Black women from the category "woman." Most Black women would only gain voting rights five decades later, thanks to Black feminist liberation struggle; the fight against racist disenfranchisement goes on. Rowling and co. would of course reject any such charges of racism—they claim to support the rights of all women, at least those they count as women. But trans exclusion cannot be disentangled from the white supremacist project of strict sex categorization and gender enforcement.

"Feminists can aim for semantic influence over the category 'women,' " writes Heyes, "and redefine its boundaries with the explicit acknowledgment that this is a political activity (not an unproblematically 'objective' scientific or medical one) within which power differentials affect the semantic authority of the participants, including different women."

It's simply not the case, and this is an empirical point, that sense gets lost when we say, "Trans women are women." I would have to try extremely hard, would have to contort and wrestle with my use and understanding of the word "woman" and when to apply it, were I to want to consistently exclude trans women. And indeed, it is the anti-trans zealots who are often tying themselves in knots, struggling to bend the world to their taxonomical convictions. The consequences can be dire: women both cis and trans have been attacked in the street by extremists obsessed with identifying and eradicating anyone they feel should not count as a woman.

Basic respect for human life and dignity requires that we refer to people according to their preferences. And here's the thing: it's easy to do so and make sense. Even if it sometimes takes a little practice. (I've made mistakes; if I misgender someone by using the wrong pronoun, I apologize, correct myself, do better next time.) Our language games—our activities of making sense—*do* lend themselves most readily to practices of trans affirmation.

But this is where the work of political struggle comes in; here is where we must address the problem of power. Because we don't all get to make meaning equally; it's not a democratic process. Powerful media corporations, social media leviathans, governments, pharmaco-medical institutions, cops, judges, other varied institutions of power—they have greater leverage to monopolize some of the most fraught words in our vocabularies: criminal, threat, crazy, swarm, terrorist. And there can be no doubt about the ferocity with which trans eliminationists will fight to stamp out forms of life that challenge gender conformity.

AT THE END of Walsh's nasty little film, certainty and self-evident common sense are supposedly delivered when Walsh asks his wife, "What is a woman?" She replies, "An adult human female," and then asks her husband to help her to open a jar of pickles. It is an unwitting directorial slip on Walsh's part, admitting that gender indeed functions as a set of activities and practices, not captured by an oh-so-simple definition. "Adult human female" is nonetheless a definition-cum-slogan regurgitated by both anti-trans conservatives and trans-exclusionary feminists as a gesture to a certain notion of biological determinism.

What does it mean to say an "adult human female" is definitively what a woman is? The purported definition is, notably, not a guide that we ever use to learn, apply and master the use of the word "woman" in the actual world. Children learn the word "woman," and adequately and meaningfully use it in their lives all the time, without first having to learn the concept of "adult human female" (whatever such a process would look like—we don't know, because we don't do it). Indeed, we do not teach children how to use the word "woman" by teaching them to first identify adult human females. We, collectively, use the word "woman" in language, and children pick up this practice accordingly. Non-English speakers do not learn what "woman" means in English by first learning what "adult human female" means.

But since high-profile anti-trans figures seem so convinced that this is a game those of us who challenge gender and sex essentialism will lose, let's provisionally accept the definition "adult human female." Why should a trans woman not fall under the category adult human female, simply because she was not assigned female at birth? The transphobe might argue that trans women are not biological females, as they cannot bear children or produce eggs. But what about women, cis and assigned female at birth, who are physically unable to ovulate? Not female? Surely, the transphobe would not want their definition to exclude such women.

We could keep going: What about the woman who is assigned female at birth, has all visible typically female sex characteristics, but learns at some point that she, too, has XY chromosomes and internal testes? Or those with XXY chromosomes? Are such women to be moved into the not-woman category? Or what about intersex babies born with ambiguous genitalia? (We know in such cases, doctors would historically, and still regularly do, decide whether to deem the baby a boy or girl, and operate accordingly.)

The key point is, at every turn, when reactionaries and gender conformity ideologues attempt to give a simple answer by invoking biology, their definition falls short in covering all the cases where even they would want to use the term "woman," *and* it doesn't do what they want in terms of cleanly excluding trans women. That is, "adult human female" does not do the definitional work that the anti-trans lobby wants it to do, because all they really desire is grounds for their exclusionary agenda. The definition doesn't provide that, and a simple definition it is not.

It's telling that anti-trans campaigners must continue to find new language to cling to, to push an exclusionary binary, when a chosen biological definition fails to draw the clean line between men and women that they wish it did.

On his first day back in office, for example, Donald Trump signed an executive order aimed at eradicating trans and gender-nonconforming people. It was unconstitutional, of course, and also unscientific nonsense. The order defined "female" and "male" as follows: " 'Female' means a person belonging, at conception, to the sex that produces the large reproductive cell . . . 'Male' means a person belonging, at conception, to the sex that produces the small reproductive cell."

Observers were swift to note that by adding "at conception," the order bundles in a notion of fetal personhood—a nod to the fact that attacks on gender nonconformity are part and parcel of a pronatalist agenda that attacks all reproductive freedoms. It is no accident that the definitions of "female" and "male" are centered solely on reproductive function. The definition is also senseless; at conception, embryos are not sexually differentiated. And at conception, fetuses are also not producing reproductive cells, or gametes, large or small. But the definition need not make scientific or practical sense to appease gender conformity fanatics.

If the language of sex-qua-reproductive-cells was odd to see on a presidential document, it was nothing new to the anti-trans lobby. Anti-trans ideologues glom on to the language of gametes because their previous reliance on chromosomes—XX and XY—permitted too many examples outside the chromosomal binary to contend with. Gametes seemed to do the trick for those transphobes who demand that sex be understood as strictly binary.

Firstly, again, not everyone produces reproductive cells. There are many cis women who do not produce large reproductive cells, or ova. When this is pointed out, the common transphobe response is that these women are atypical, and that these women *would* produce ova were it not for some sort of dysfunction.

That is, the anti-trans appeal to biological reality must rely on a fictional biological world in which all bodies develop in precisely predetermined ways—and those ways are designed toward reproduction. It's an inherently conservative, indeed religious, view of bodily function and predestiny. “There is nothing that bodies ‘ought’ to do in the absence of doing it, because bodily functionality is evolved, not designed,” the advocate and author Kim Hipwell writes, countering the bizarre modal logic deployed by transphobes to claim that all women *would* be producers of large reproductive cells. “Evolution has no foresight, no goals that it is planning to achieve—and nor do its products. They are not ‘set up to’ do anything. The apparent ‘design’ that is embodied in organisms is a mirage: to argue otherwise is to engage in creationism.”

In the actual world, this gamete definition would also discount a good number of people the transphobes themselves would classify as women or female. Anti-trans bigots have always had a clear vision of who they would like to exclude from the category of womanhood, but this distinction was never based on observing which bodies do or do not produce large reproductive cells.

The anti-trans speaker who invokes biological reality might stubbornly insist that the only acceptable definition of “human female,” and thus “woman,” is a person with XX chromosomes or a producer of large gametes. Such an answer appeals to those who demand that sex be understood as immutable—they seek something bodily that cannot be changed. Secondary sex characteristics like breasts and certain distributions of body hair, hormone levels and shape of genitalia are not so clearly split between all those assigned female and male at birth. Crucially, these are also sex traits that trans people can indeed obtain: one can change gender, yes, but even though one cannot change chromosomal makeup, one *can* change sex (biological sex characteristics, traits). I have seen people do it, and so have many if not most of you. “I’ve done it,” Grace Lavery recently quipped on a podcast, and she has. The distinction between sex and gender was, after all, only “invented by researchers in the late 20th century to describe different aspects of people that may not all align in the same person," as biologist and trans activist Julia Serano has noted.

It gets worse still, philosophically, for the transphobes, should they want to say that the meaning of the word "woman" should essentially be reduced to chromosomes or gametes (which, I repeat, would exclude numerous women assigned female at birth): they must admit in turn that, for the most part, when they use the word "woman" in the world, they can't be sure that they're using it correctly. If they want to insist on such a definition, they themselves, and everyone who learns the word "woman"—and manages to correctly and successfully communicate using that word in the world without knowing shit about chromosomes—could in fact be wrongly applying the word every time they unwittingly apply it to someone who does not have XX chromosomes or does not produce ova. This would have been happening for centuries, of course, as talk of chromosomes only began in the late nineteenth century, and Karl Ernst von Baer only discovered the mammalian ovum in 1827. Are they then to say that, since these biological posits were not yet discovered, prior to then, without this alleged definition of the term "woman," it was only by guessing that the word was ever correctly used? Since we don't directly perceive chromosomes or gametes or talk about them when talking about women, except in extremely specific and rare medical circumstances, recognizing someone as an "XX chromosome haver" or "large gamete producer" cannot be definitive of how we correctly use the word "woman."

This is no problem for those of us who rightly reject the definition game. It is the anti-trans camp's insistence that correct usage of the word "woman" requires the ability to provide its definition. It is they who assert that we have to know the definition and be able to use it as a guide in order to determine when to correctly call a person a "woman." But in using their alleged definition of woman, they must forgo their claim to correct usage on their very own terms; they cannot offer a simple definition that is either non-circular, coherent, or a guide for when they use the term "woman" in daily life. But wasn't it the transphobes' contention that *only* they were able to use the term correctly? Wasn't that the basis of the "define woman" gotcha?

The transphobe has one last gambit: "Well, sure," they might respond, "we don't go around testing chromosomes or gametes before using the word 'woman,' but we do know we use the term correctly, because such testing is possible." This logic goes along the lines of: we don't test every given person's chromosomes, but we *could*, and thus it is technically knowable whether someone is *really* a woman.

This is no idle threat: so-called sex testing in professional athletics has a violent, racist, decades-long history, worsened in these times of anti-trans backlash. In what Human Rights Watch calls "practices that violate fundamental rights to privacy and dignity," sports governing bodies have overwhelmingly selected successful Black athletes for invasive chromosomal, hormone and genital testing, in order to potentially exclude them from competing. As *New York Times Magazine* writer Ruth Padawer notes in an extensive feature on the practice, endocrinologists and geneticists have for decades challenged the delineations and exclusions sex-testing purports to achieve: "Relying on science to arbitrate the male-female divide in sports is fruitless, they said, because science could not draw a line that nature itself refused to draw." Not that this has mattered to the regulating bodies and gender-conformity zealots, committed as they are to the brutal colonialist legacy of gender ontologizing and to excluding Black women from the category of woman.

Meanwhile, so rabid is the Republican effort to eliminate trans children—and all trans people—from public life, that laws proposed in Ohio, Kansas, and New Jersey, among other US states, to ban trans girls from sports, have opened the door to genital testing requirements on girls whose assigned sex at birth is questioned. And to be clear, genital, hormone and chromosomal testing has nothing to do with discovering the "truth" of someone's sex, as is purported; rather, it is through these violent discourses and practices that reactionaries hold fast to eliminationist categories of gender and sex, drawing and upholding such boundaries as they go.

In roughly the past five years, nearly 1,000 anti-trans bills have been introduced in state legislatures across the US, and these are echoed in Republican federal efforts. Numerous states bar trans students from playing sports, bar trans children from accessing the correct bathrooms, and ban discussions of sexual orientation or gender identity in schools. At least twenty-seven states have some form of ban on minors accessing gender-affirming care. Florida and Texas led the way in passing laws with devious mechanisms around medical liability, insurance provision and procedural hurdles to render transition-related healthcare inaccessible for adults, too. Trump's early executive orders expunged the mention of the T and the Q from LGBTQ on all federal government websites, and his orders ruled that all passports and federal government identification paperwork identify people only with their sex assigned at birth.

Beyond statehouses and courtrooms, the right wing has declared open season on LBGTQ spaces. It is now common practice for armed, self-identifying Christian nationalist militia members to harass family-friendly drag brunches and drag queen story hours.

This is the very meaning of eliminationism: a political project aimed at the thoroughgoing exclusion of trans and other gender nonconforming people from public life.

When held up to legal scrutiny in federal court challenges, numerous anti-trans laws were found to be unconstitutional by even conservative judges from Florida to Tennessee to Arkansas, and—perhaps more importantly—these rulings have agreed that arguments treating gender-affirming treatments for youths as untested and dangerous are, quite simply, not based in fact. Regardless, Republicans have made clear that they plan to brute force their eliminationist assault on trans people into legal reality. Whatever relief we might rightly feel when pernicious laws are blocked, the far right knows how to bend legal paradigms to their will through tireless and well-funded campaigns, working through the minority rule of Republican-led statehouses until eventually reaching the extreme right-wing Supreme Court. The same playbook—written by the same think tanks and astroturfed across state houses—hacked away at abortion access until an established constitutional right was wholly overturned and settled law was ripped to shreds. When bathroom bans were first introduced in red-state legislatures like Nevada's a decade ago, they roundly failed to get off the ground; now they are law in vast swaths of the country.

Democrats failed for decades to vigorously defend reproductive rights by lending all too much credence to the Christian right's anti-abortion stance. President Bill Clinton's famous phrase—that abortion should be "safe, legal, and rare"—treated abortion as an unfortunate necessity rather than an integral part of bodily autonomy and a public good. There's a relevant analogy here with the common liberal treatment of trans kids: that they're an unfortunate rarity, which should be tolerated but not celebrated.

Against such a threadbare defense of trans existence, the violently committed anti-trans right will surely prevail. Liberals putatively opposed to the right's draconian anti-trans onslaught should take heed of the judges' rulings on trans youth healthcare. All too many powerful liberal organs—the *New York Times* perhaps chief among them—have channeled Republican talking points by treating trans children as a site of peril, and gender-affirming treatment for kids as potentially too experimental.

In point after point, however, federal court rulings *rejected* arguments that claim gender-affirming treatments for youths are untested and unsafe. "What is clear is that before all kinds of judges, when these bans are tested by what the states are claiming is their evidence, they categorically fail," ACLU attorney and trans advocate Chase Strangio told me in an interview. "What that means is that you have a popular discourse playing far more hostile to trans people, far more open to misinformation, than a federal court is at this stage." Strangio added that "it would be helpful if the center left media were to then cover the cases, after having sparked fear everywhere." Liberals might not be echoing conservative groomer conspiracies, but anti-trans panic abounds, reliably articulated by liberals as fear for the fates of children—notional children, who are presumed cis and invariably white.

So let's talk about children. I don't remember learning the words "woman" or "man" as a child, do you? The process, I mean, by which we learned to use the terms in the world. Certainly any early childhood utterances would have been practiced with just a few examples, in only so many language games. I don't intend anything nostalgic here. I mean, do you remember learning "woman," "man," or "boy," "girl"—what did it involve? I wonder how anyone can observe children learning to do things with words and fail to notice the contingent nature, through training, with which certain concepts build up, connect and calcify for them. As Wittgenstein notes, "The child learns to believe a host of things. I.e. it learns to act according to these beliefs. Bit by bit there forms a system of what is believed, and in that system some things stand unshakeably fast and some are more or less liable to shift.

A few years ago, when my nephew must have been three or four, he told me, "When I'm big, I'm going to be a mummy." I responded that this was a lovely plan. "And," he continued, "when Mummy is bigger, she is going to be a big Daddy." It made perfect sense from where he stood, his life populated by only so many characters: people grew, this he knew; my brother, his dad, was the biggest person in the household, so that's what his mother, the second biggest, would surely become. And he, too, would grow through the Mummy stage.

Such thinking didn't last long, and my nephew wasn't revealing any special "from the mouths of babes" understanding of gender's porousness; his rudimentary taxonomy of gender variance illustrated only this: that it takes training and practice to see the world as carved up in a certain way.

Inculcation into a gendered world starts so young—the declarative "it's a girl" or "it's a boy" was made about most of us before we were named—it should come as no surprise that a gender binary functions for so many as a world-ordering certainty, immune from doubt, outside of which they cannot think; a regime beyond a schema. A hinge. How remarkable then, what proof of undeniable and dazzling *Dasein*, in a world so ordered from birth, that there are trans and nonbinary kids and adults at all. And how shameful that some so-called progressives and nearly every mainstream liberal newspaper treat the fact of more trans kids coming out as something to fear or avoid. As if there could be too many!

Time and again, I've heard ostensibly well-meaning liberals regurgitate the same sentences about trans kids that have previously been used to treat homosexuality, or interracial couples, as sites of potential peril. The refrain is the same: I support trans rights, but won't children suffer? And the answer should be the same: Trans kids are not new; transness is only a condition of suffering if we maintain a world wherein such identities and relationships are deemed unnatural and unwanted. "What would it take for you to actively wish for and want there to be trans people in the world?" challenged Gill-Peterson in an interview. "Not just to accepting that there are trans kids or saying that they should technically be allowed to survive into adulthood. That's the bare minimum. What would it look like to celebrate and welcome them into the world and to say that, 'We're happy that you're here? I want you to be here'?"

That liberal discourse instead tends to treat transness as a condition to be at best tolerated speaks to what I want to call cis certainty. It is among the world-ordering certainties (in the Wittgensteinian sense) to which we fail to attend and question as such. It seems uncontroversial to note that assumptions of cis conformity structure contemporary life—a historically produced fact forged in five hundred years of colonialist hegemony. As we've addressed, this does not reflect the existence of some special gendered essences running through our beings.

As a cis woman, I didn't ever *learn the truth* of my gender, my sex, because I didn't need to. I don't mean for a second that it was some innate internal essence to which I've always had access. Leave behind talk of innateness—no one should be required to feel "born this way" to live and flourish in and through the gender expression(s) they desire. Rather, I did not learn my gender because in a world in which cisness is presumed, a cis person's gender identity is not the result of knowledge acquisition. It just so happens that I've almost never felt alienation in performing the gender I was assigned at birth; I don't know what it feels like to be trans or nonbinary. But acquiring and developing such embodied habits and sensibilities of cis womanhood are not activities of developing a justified true belief (knowledge) about oneself. Philosopher Megan Burke calls this "cis sense—a particular way a norm of cis-ness circulates and animates gendered meaning in our lives." It is the work of certainty. Which, Wittgenstein reminds us, is not grounded in some deeper truth that we come to *know*. Our language games, notes Wittgenstein, are just "there—like our life": cisness *gets* to just be in ways transness does not.

Transness is consistently subjected to suspicion. Doubt around trans people's claims and desires, particularly those of trans children, serves as a constant mechanism for invalidating trans experience, denying necessary care, ensuring marginalization and (particularly for Black and brown trans people) criminalization and violence. In order to access treatments, trans individuals are required to perform near-absolute self-knowledge about their gender identities, a knowledge never demanded of cis people—if I wanted to get my breasts enhanced, I would have to perform no such knowledge of my being-woman, or being much of anything except able to pay. I've been on the contraceptive pill (hormones) since I was fourteen, no questions asked. This points to how cisness functions as an organizing certainty.

Cisness is not treated as a site of doubt, but it isn't a site of knowledge, either. When trans people are aggressively doubted, it is within a hinge epistemology of cisness. But by functioning as a certainty, cisness does not have some greater metaphysical standing; it's just a sedimented practice—a traceable, historically situated formation, resistant to doubt but unsupported by further grounds. If transness introduces doubt, it is because (unlike cisness) it makes sense to talk about trans knowledge. Trans-suspicious thinking (poor philosophy) frames transness as a terrain of unending, dangerous uncertainty; what this forgets is that where there can be doubt, there can be knowledge. Cis certainty, meanwhile, cannot function as knowledge; it forecloses terrains of questioning, of knowledge.

Rather, in a world where cisness is treated as (enforced as) natural, forms of life that challenge this dominant framework involve the activity of knowing, of becoming expert. It should not be controversial to note that those who do not experience normalized formations of gender and sex as givens are in a position to know more. And it is through such expertise, such wisdom, that trans people have been able to survive and navigate, including the navigation of suspicious and doubting medical gatekeepers; it's something akin to Du Bois's notion of the "second-sight" with which Black people have (are forced to have) knowledge about and beyond the "veil" of a white world to survive in it. Trans knowledge is an aperture through which gender is doubted, learned, and practiced otherwise; this should, much like Judith Butler's framing of gender as performance, serve to dislodge cis certainty. That it rarely does—that it is individual trans people, rather than cisness in general, who are subjected to doubt when cis normativity is challenged—reflects how very anchoring cis sense remains in dominant discourse.

Cis certainty is produced and reproduced as that hinge of gender binarism and segmented productive and reproductive labor, cemented in the traditional nuclear family, on which contemporary relations of production hang. Despite ancient, unbroken histories of gender nonconformity across cultures, despite trans kids having existed for centuries, cisness is maintained as certain. Well-meaning trans-supportive liberals who think transphobia is principally a matter of innocent ignorance—that people just don't know enough—should pay better attention to the ferocity of today's fascistic, organized anti-trans backlash, and to the wealth of life-ordering activities that hold cis certainty in place.

Specific, institutionalized practices of doubting help uphold this status quo. As historian Beans Velocci has pointed out, the history of trans medicine and legislating gender identity is a history organized through particular uncertainties: not uncertainty about the nature of sex and gender, but uncertainty about the outcomes of gender-affirming treatment and potential repercussions for medical practitioners. In the 1950s and early 1960s, endocrinologist and sexologist Harry Benjamin, celebrated as the "father" of transexual medicine, and his colleague Elmer Belt corresponded about which of their patients should or should not be approved for genital surgery—decision-making processes that later informed the formal standards of care that guide transition-related medical practices today. As Velocci notes:

> Benjamin defined transsexuality primarily through a desire for medical transition, but merely being a transsexual in this definition did not automatically result in surgical eligibility. Benjamin and Belt remained preoccupied with the possibility that transsexuals would regret their surgeries and seek legal or personal revenge, and thus their assessments of who should have surgery focused more on the possibility of a bad outcome than adherence to gender norms or classification as transsexual . . . Throughout their correspondence and clinical practice, the

> transsexual emerged as a threat to medical providers, and a subject incapable of making their own bodily decisions, needing to be protected from themselves.

While contemporary anti-trans narratives fixate on infirm taxonomical claims, these medical practitioners, Velocci explains, weren't concerned with whether a patient was *really* trans; rather, they "constructed transsexuality as a space of uncertainty through their fear-based practices and used that uncertainty to maintain clinical control . . . This fear of the future had a material legacy as trans medicine coalesced around a model that functioned as if disaster were imminent." In turn, trans people have been forced to jump over extraordinary hurdles to receive treatment readily available to cis people. They must offer proof and surety, they must perform activities of (en)gendered certainty, while being denied the very treatments and procedures that would make acting with such certainty possible in this world; doctors and psychologists and insurance companies have every leverage to deem the performance insufficient.

The idea that transness is a risk, particularly when it comes to trans minors, continues to undergird medical gatekeeping, anti-trans legislation and the transphobic panic given credence in every major broadsheet. Nowhere is the fear of possible future regret so weaponized as with trans-related healthcare. Medical liability is just one of the recent tools that far-right think tanks have turned to as devious legislative ways to ban gender-affirming healthcare while skirting constitutional protections. A bill passed in the Texas Senate, yet to become law, would make doctors and insurers strictly liable for covering the costs of any future healthcare a patient might seek throughout their entire life, should it relate to the gender-affirming care they've received. Such strict liability is wholly unprecedented and does not exist for any other medical procedures, even though a vast number of surgeries and medical treatments carry the risk of requiring future, related care. The sheer possibility of lifetime liability would make it impossible for healthcare providers to obtain the insurance coverage necessary to offer gender-affirming care. The risk would be deemed too high.

When it comes to trans kids, narratives of uncertainty and risk are fiercer still. Moral panic drips from the pages of so-called objective *New York Times* reporting on trans minors' healthcare: the coverage treats cis certainty as a silent premise; it assumes an endangered being who must be protected from transness— the Child, or what queer theorist Lee Edelman calls the "the fantasmic beneficiary of every political intervention." The Child does not exist, but conservatives are obsessed with nonexistent children. This is nothing new: The paranoia about spectral children is a central tenet of modern American conservatism. The right worries about a zygote or embryo as if it were already a child (it is not). Then there was the whole generation of nonexistent bad children whose brains turned to fried eggs on marijuana. The murderous Satanic children and the Black "superpredator" children were powerful conservative fantasies, too. The fascist figuration of the imperiled white, cis child now takes center stage in a putrid debate over trans existence. People who don't exist are far better suited to cynical political manipulation and prurient psychological projection than are living, breathing children with lives that should get to richly matter. As feminist theorist Sophie Lewis put it, "the criminalization of life-in-particular in the name of 'life itself.' "

Great harm has been done, and continues to be done, to existing children in the name of the figurative child. In the media and in statehouses, as well as in Congress, living young people are forced to argue for their existence in front of cold and calculating political bodies. "Why should some guy who has never met me, why should he get to tell me what I can and can't do?" seventeen-year-old Cyrus Hall, a trans boy, told NPR as his state of Alabama passed bills that outlawed his hormone treatment. "Why does he get to decide what is right for people who just want to be happy?" Trans children are ejected from public life and forced to live in suicidal anguish. "Little reaches more nauseating contradiction in the colonial and capitalist present than the putative care for children," Gill-Peterson notes in *Parapraxis* magazine.

In that magazine's same issue, writer Max Fox perfectly captures the operations of cis certainty at play in the frenzy around trans kids:

> This panic . . . conveys a number of presumed certainties that run together: that talking about sex is sexual activity, that gender nonconformity is sexual perversion, that children have a fixed gender but no sexuality, that to recognize someone's gender is to be implicated in it, and that trans people cannot be children. The panic is not about ignorance or uncertainty, then, but about the demand, in the panic-stricken adult's mind, to give the answer to a question they believe should go without saying . . . For a participant in the current panic, the image of the child allegedly groomed by teachers when asked for their pronouns is an affront not to trans children, certainly, nor to cis children, who seem generally quite eager to refer to people the way they request, but to that adult's desire for all children to be cis.

It's no accident that the right calls upon the myth of imperiled children to warn of trans "indoctrination," grooming, or "social contagion," with clear notions of "purity" and traditionalist family reproduction at play. In the struggle for trans rights, all too many liberals—and some leftists—have echoed notions about pure and innocent children who must be somehow protected from transness. That is, through reactionary fixations on transness as uncertainty, violent cis certainty has been held stable in the service of fascism's child. "Maybe," as Velocci suggests, when it comes to the human activity of gender and sex expression, "uncertainty is not a dirty word."

4
Seeing-As

For it is not light that is needed, but fire.

Frederick Douglass, "What to the Slave Is the Fourth of July?"

I HAVE A duck-rabbit picture tattooed on my forearm—an image that can be correctly seen as either a duck or a rabbit, but not as both at the same time. So I play the following game a lot. First a person might see a duck; I invite them to keep looking. "Do you see anything else?" "Oh, wow, now I see a rabbit!" The image itself hasn't changed when the rabbit appears to them, nor have the basic processes of visual perception, but, as Wittgenstein describes it, a new "aspect" of the image "dawns" on the viewer; they are "struck" by it. What has changed is the viewer's relation to the object, her ability to see it as something, and then as something else.

"Could there be human beings lacking in the capacity to see something as something—and what would that be like?" Wittgenstein asks in the *Philosophical Investigations*. "What sort of consequences would it have?"

Seeing something *as something*. Like seeing marks on a piece of paper as a picture of something, a drawing of a smiley face as a smiling face, a series of lines as a word. We might see a landscape as spooky, or suddenly see a family resemblance in two siblings' faces that we hadn't previously noticed. The most famous example Wittgenstein used is that of the duck-rabbit picture.

Wittgenstein, as was typical for the philosopher, was making no political or ethical allusions as he unpacked his thinking on "seeing-as." But there are significant political stakes in answering Wittgenstein's question in the positive—yes, *there can be human beings lacking in the capacity to see something as something*.

Wittgenstein's reflections are not just idle points about Gestalt puzzles but the relational and collective nature of perception in general. To be struck by a new aspect (rabbit), you have to see the image as something (duck) in the first place. There is also something deeply social in our constant activities of perceiving. We might not all respond to perceptual stimuli in the exact same way. (Consider Rorschach tests, or the different ways differently neurodivergent people might respond to subtle facial expressions, for example.) But, by and large, we find shared points of judgment when we see something as something. Seeing-as, therefore, is not a free-for-all. If someone looked at my duck-rabbit tattoo and said something like, "Oh, now I see it is a tree! . . . Now I see it is the devil!" I would wonder if they were high, or needed glasses. The duck-rabbit is, in fact, a drawing of a duck and/or a rabbit.

We might see different images emerge in cloud formations or paint splatter, but we invite each other to share in seeing the aspects when they dawn on us, and these others are often successful in doing so. We might feel baffled or bemused, meanwhile, when someone says they can't see what we so clearly see—that's the pleasure of the game. The least interesting things about these perception games are the physical attributes of the image, the visual stimuli; the puzzles are interesting only in the ways we relate to them socially, with each other.

If I say, "Meet me under the sign for the station," or "Pass me ten dollars," or "Don't speak to the cop," such commands require a lot of shared judgment on seeing-as to be successfully followed. Both interlocutors must see the green and white rectangle of paper as ten dollars, for example, to successfully pass each other the money.

Now, to Wittgenstein's question: "Could there be human beings lacking in the capacity to see something as something?"

To stay with our classic example for a minute: we might imagine a person unable to ever see the rabbit aspect of the duck-rabbit image, however long they looked at the image. Perhaps this person has had no previous encounters with rabbits or images of rabbits. In such a case, simply giving them more and more information about the duck-rabbit picture does not enable the rabbit aspect to dawn on them. Instead, they need certain things in the context of their life outside this game to change: they need to experience some rabbits, even if just in photos or children's books. This is a frivolous and weird example, but the point is that aspect perception of any sort (seeing something *as something*) involves experience in a shared world of reference. And that's no less true for other forms of sense perception: to hear a given series of sounds *as* a specific word with a given meaning in a language and a context requires particular experiences and training in a shared form of life.

It is very difficult to imagine someone who, even with all the necessary rabbit-related background and references, is never able to see the duck-rabbit image as a rabbit. Or someone who, with all the seemingly relevant linguistic training, is never able to perceive the meaning of a given expression. Such immutable "aspect blindness," as Wittgenstein describes this inability, might be something like color blindness but far weirder, for it would not be attributable to the viewer's physical makeup. Although notably, a colorblind person only discovers themselves to be colorblind once they're socialized in a world with color language and references to color; in a practical sense, you can't be colorblind alone. As philosopher Gordon Baker noted, "Nobody can establish by himself that he is blind to an aspect."

But here's the real problem, and the reason I'm talking about duck-rabbits and perception puzzles: The notion of "human beings lacking in the capacity to see something as something" is not really so alien to us at all. We are constantly faced with brutal examples of human beings apparently lacking in the capacity to see certain other human beings as fully human.

I'm not talking about the small percentage of people who might be diagnosed with an antisocial personality disorder. My interest here is not psychopathology in any clinical sense. I'm talking about the significant number of people who appear to share most every perceptual, psychological and emotional capacity to see humans as humans. They have friends and loved ones they care about; they might cry at sad films or be moved by the news of certain people's suffering. And they are seeing what we're seeing. For example, we have observed all too many people watch the same scenes we have seen of parents in Gaza carrying the shreds of their slaughtered children's bodies, but they are not seeing *as* we are seeing. In all their responses and subsequent actions to defend Israel, it becomes quite clear that they are not seeing Palestinians as fully human.

An extrapolation from the duck-rabbit image to the dehumanization of whole groups of people is an extreme leap, I know. But we must take seriously the ways that supremacist ideology involves practices of perception and recognition. Philosopher Stanley Cavell, borrowing directly from Wittgenstein's idea of aspect-blindness, described the condition of someone unable to see another person as fully human as something like a "soul blindness."

The term "soul-blind" is not perfect—after all, it denotes a moral failure, not any medical condition or impairment. Cavell's concept is helpful, though, in specifically calling upon Wittgenstein's sense of aspect blindness to show why you cannot simply correct a soul-blind person with more evidence of what they're already observing. Like in cases of aspect blindness, states of soul blindness are not readily shifted by pointing at the same thing again and again and demanding, "But don't you see?" If someone looks at ninety-nine duck-rabbit images and can never see the rabbit, showing them yet another duck-rabbit image is unlikely to do the trick. You might consider changing your approach. Yet in the face of violent, unchanging soul blindness, all too many of us keep expecting the same games of exposure to work. We fail to attend to the entrenched certainties that perpetuate soul blindness along lines of historic and systematic oppression; we fail to attend to what holds those certainties in place. Soul blindness is not a problem of insufficient information or evidence.

NEARLY THREE MONTHS passed between the date of Ahmaud Arbery's death in February 2020 and the indictment of his killers on murder charges that May. Arbery, a twenty-five-year-old Black man, was shot dead while jogging near his home in Brunswick, Georgia. He was hunted by George McMichael and his son, Travis—two white men—who chased Arbery in their truck. We know exactly how the lynching occurred, because McMichael's neighbor, William Bryan (also white), filmed the whole thing on his phone. His documentation was not an effort to hold the lynchers accountable; Bryan had jumped in his truck and joined the hunt. He framed the young jogger in his phone's sights while his neighbor did the same with a shotgun. They agreed on how they saw Arbery, what they saw him as.

At first, local authorities declined to charge the men. It was only when Bryan's video went public, prompting a mass outcry, that the Georgia Bureau of Investigations opened a case. The men were arrested within a day. Back then, I wrote that "it took no less than the intolerable spectacle of a Black man's execution in public view, spread far and wide, for the state to consider—or be compelled to consider—even the possibility of consequences for those who so readily took his life." And technically, that was true: there was a chain of events linking the lynching video's release and the killers' convictions. All three white men were convicted of murder by the state of Georgia and found guilty of federal hate crimes charges.

Scholar and writer Zoé Samudzi responded at the time that there was no element of justice possible in this series of events: "If the argument is that witnessing this violence is enough or is necessary to galvanize action, my single question is when? When will these acts become too unacceptable to simply continue to watch? In how many more decades, and after how many more dead?" The witnessing of racist atrocities, specifically white people observing anti-Black terror, has never served as an intervention to white supremacist violence—indeed, white witnessing has always been a constitutive part of lynchings. After the Civil War, photographs of lynchings were published as postcards, which were circulated and kept as souvenirs by white Americans. The distribution of lynching postcards through the United States Postal Service was only banned in 1908.

"We've seen antebellum images of enslaved black people whose backs were marred by whip marks, we've seen Bill Hudson's photographs of black protesters being attacked by high-powered fire hoses and police dogs at the command of Bull Connor," Samudzi wrote; we've seen such horrors for decades. White witnesses like me have seen enough to be fully aware of what's going on.

Meanwhile, Samudzi noted, the allegedly sympathetic circulation of images and videos of public violence itself performs a status-quo-upholding function. For "self-identified white progressives or leftists," she wrote,

> the videos reassure them of the statis [*sic*] of their subject-position, while their public affronted pearl-clutching at and condemnation of the filmed horrors permits them to claim moral-political superiority over other whites. It allows for action without disruption. A reassuring sameness.

I wanted to respond to Samudzi that *of course* I agree, and the passage of events—lynching, mass viewing, rare trial, rare conviction, repeat—is not a story of justice, let alone a story in which justice is delivered by white viewers and their dismayed reposts, or, indeed, by the US carceral system. But such defensiveness would have belied my participation in the ritual that Samudzi had rightly denounced.

The practice of the dutiful white witness in Arbery's case was just that, a ritual, which in and of itself changes nothing in the structure of our necropolitical racist order. Without an answer to the scholar's questions—"When will these acts become too unacceptable to simply continue to watch? In how many more decades, and after how many more dead?"—there was nothing to add. Two weeks after Abery's killers were arrested, George Floyd was murdered by the Minneapolis police; that footage circulated, too.

"If all of the evidence over the last 200 years that Black witnesses have put together doesn't convince you that there is a systemic problem of anti-Black racism in the country, then no amount of video will," journalism professor Allison Richardson said on the legal podcast *Amicus* in 2020. She recalled questioning some of her white friends who had said they were watching the Floyd murder video to "educate" themselves on the issue. "When white people die—violently, we don't ask for video," she added.

Nationwide rebellions followed Floyd's murder, breaking through the isolations and differentially distributed terrors of the first pandemic summer. But it would make little sense to say that the uprisings were a response to enough people having, finally, *seen enough* after watching Floyd beg for his life and gasp his last breaths under Officer Derek Chauvin's knee.

The reasons things kicked off as they did and when they did—and as opposed to in the wake of another brutal and virally shared lynching video—is hard to fully determine. The spark was not, however, lit by online observers expressing outrage and sharing the video but arguably by the brave rebels who burned down the Minneapolis Police Department's Third Precinct three days after Floyd's killing. I watched the precinct burn via livestream video, and I joined thousands of others in the streets of Brooklyn the next night—and for many days and nights after that. The point was not to bear witness; the feeling was that something else seemed (albeit for a short time) almost possible. A new aspect dawned, fleetingly displacing a picture of racist police power.

How many more dead? The number of people killed by police every year in the US has only risen since 2020, and it remains the case that a disproportionate number of those killed are Black. It is not for lack of evidence that this continues.

There are many stories that can be and have been told about the white supremacist backlash against the George Floyd uprisings. Much has been rightly said, too, about the force of liberal defanging, cooptation, and cowardice—the swiftness with which they softened and then erased the abolitionist calls at the heart of the rebellions. The fractured left also bears its own responsibilities for failures on multiple fronts to take up and continue the uprisings' militant challenge to racial capitalism.

It tells us something, though, that it was only following the mass unrest that far right forces escalated their push to stop schools from teaching about the US's racist history and present. The Manhattan Institute's Christopher Rufo began his campaign against the openly manufactured boogeyman of "critical race theory" in late summer 2020. At no point did the architects of "anti-woke" white panic like Rufo call for the videos of police lynchings to be taken down. Their followers used the videos for sport.

"I began to see memes popping up . . . I saw white men posed like George Floyd, with the knee on the neck and pretending to be officer Chauvin," the journalist Richardson said. "I thought: Everyone is not looking at this through a similar lens."

TAKE ANOTHER example. Israel's genocide has produced images of mutilated Palestinian children, scenes of shuddering grief, starvation, obliteration and relentless death, not to mention the spectacle of Israeli soldiers taking annihilatory pleasure, as a constant part of so many of our social media feeds. The injunction—don't look away, all eyes on Gaza—prompts Samudzi's question again, "When will these acts become too unacceptable to simply continue to watch?" The many indifferent or even celebratory responses to images from Gaza offer a stinging answer to Wittgenstein's query, "Could there be human beings lacking in the capacity to see something as something?"

Millions of pairs of eyes saw—asynchronously, by way of social media—footage of a Palestinian man grasping the headless body of his one-year-old baby son, Ahmad, after Israel demolished Rafah in May 2024. My wonderful student, also called Ahmad, escaped Gaza before the Rafah pass closed that spring.

Israeli strikes on his family home on October 9, 2023, killed his mother and sister. As the genocide proceeded, he updated me every time another of his family was slaughtered. "How can I live?" he asked me in a text message, under a picture of two little corpses covered in gray dust: his cousins, both under ten years old.

Biden lied about seeing photos of beheaded Israeli babies allegedly killed on October 7. He saw no such thing, as the White House was forced to admit later, but that didn't matter. The US's unqualified backing of Israel's genocide was assured regardless. And it is not for lack of seeing, for lack of knowing, the extent of Israel's atrocities that US and broader Western complicity in the genocide continued.

Such has been the terrain of certainty and doubt in the establishment media and political discourse: Israel was accorded certainty, which was not grounded in knowledge. Again and again, unverified claims circulated: about beheaded kibbutzim babies, babies in ovens, fetuses cut from Israeli women's bodies; about Hamas headquarters under hospitals, homes, and schools; Hamas behind every doctor, journalist, and middle-aged Gazan man. No matter how many of these were debunked, Israeli forces and Western powers continued to act with genocidal certainty as if these claims were true. Those who challenged Israeli testimony were not seen as good-faith skeptics demanding proof; they were dismissed as antisemites. Meanwhile, Palestinian testimonies, livestreamed video evidence, and photos were subjected to psychotic doubt.

In 2025, Bari Weiss's Zionist news site, the Free Press, sought to cast such doubt on the firmly established fact of mass starvation in Gaza by reporting that some of the emaciated Palestinian children featured in viral images depicting the Israel-induced famine were not only starving but were also sick with preexisting conditions. The supposed gotcha was that children with disabilities and preexisting health conditions, who could not get the treatment and nutrition they needed because of Israel's siege, were not representative of the population. The photos were somehow, by this logic, unfairly maligning Israel; meanwhile, the powerful country enforced mass starvation across Gaza by policy, which it could end any day. It was, I wrote at the time, like suggesting that the Nazis didn't kill Anne Frank because she died of typhus in the Bergen-Belsen concentration camp.

A performance of doubt in which no actual route to knowledge is possible or permitted is not doubt; it simply expresses a certainty. In early October 2024, dozens of US doctors, nurses and paramedics who had volunteered in Gaza testified to having seen multiple cases of small children who had been shot in the head. "At the time, I assumed this had to be the work of a particularly sadistic soldier located nearby," said one trauma surgeon. "But after returning home, I met an emergency medicine physician who had worked in a different hospital in Gaza two months before me. 'I couldn't believe the number of kids I saw shot in the head,' I told him. To my surprise, he responded: 'Yeah, me, too. Every single day.' " This testimony, and others just like it, was published in the *New York Times*: Readers of that news organ, notorious for manufacturing consent for Israel's genocide, were faced with X-ray images of numerous tiny skulls with bullets lodged inside. A UN report later confirmed that "children, including toddlers, were shot in the head by snipers."

On the social media platform X, I saw numerous swift responses to the X-ray images, responses framed in the register of forensic expertise, asserting that the images were faked by Hamas. X-Rays of bullets in skulls, said the posters, did not look like that. Such conspiracy theorizing is common on Elon Musk's platform, and it is typically grouped under the problem of online mis/disinformation. The issue of seeing-as here is, however, more fundamental.

"They weren't looking away exactly," wrote physician and writer Mary Turfah of the "colleagues, acquaintances, talk show hosts, reporters in the West" who appeared to lack the capacity to see Palestinians as fully human in the face of a livestreamed genocide. "We shared a present and a world, in the literal sense, and as such their heads faced the same directions as ours as they went about their lives. They were seeing what the rest of us saw and looking beyond it, locking eyes with only the people in whom they recognized themselves."

This is not to suggest that it would thus have been better to stop sharing footage from Gaza. If the circulation of visual proof of Israel's war crimes were wholly pointless, I doubt its leaders would dedicate such specific focus to barring reporters from entering Gaza while systematically targeting, threatening and murdering Gazan journalists. Over 270 journalists have been killed by Israel since October 7, 2023—that's more reporters killed than in both world wars, the Vietnam War, the wars in Yugoslavia, and the war in Afghanistan combined.

Yet both these things can be true at once: that Israel, the US and complicit corporations and media outlets expend extraordinary energies and violent force in hiding and obfuscating the truth about Israel's atrocities and that the mass exposure of that truth, in its most bloody and terrible forms—in the shape of a beheaded baby, a flayed toddler, countless ashen-faced child corpses that have populated social media feeds—constructs no real hurdle to Israel's fulfilling its eliminationist ambitions.

When Palestinians demand of Western audiences, "Don't look away," no one is pretending that looking is sufficient. The assumption is that no one could witness such horror and fail to take action to stop it. And millions of people around the world were moved to action—thousands of students and workers risked arrest, expulsion, and even deportation to stand against genocidal complicity. The problem was not that a majority of people failed to see Palestinians as fully human. It was that soul blindness to Palestinians was the official stance of governments, media and cultural institutions, and universities.

For Cavell, the figure of the slave owner exemplifies a soul-blind person. In relating to Black people as property, the slave owner sees Black people as, in Cavell's words, "not purely human," not "ensouled" in the same way he imagines a person *like himself*, a white person, to be. When he sees an enslaved Black mother weeping when her children are taken from her to be sold, it is not that he is not capable of seeing the scene of a grieving human parent but that he does not see the humanity of the parent as equal to that of white parents. We hardly need examples from history: Trump supporters have created whole meme genres dedicated to mocking weeping immigrants who have been ripped from their loved ones. To be soul-blind is to fail to perceive people deemed other as part of the "same ethical and political order," as philosophers David Owen and Jonathan Havercroft put it.

The late Charles Krauthammer—a diehard Zionist *Washington Post* columnist—wrote a column titled "Moral clarity in Gaza," praising Israel's actions during its 2014 assault on Gaza, which killed over 2,000 Palestinians including over 500 children. Atrocity images circulated then, too, including photos of the mangled, limp frames of four Palestinian kids killed on a Gaza beach by Israeli missiles. Krauthammer described the children as "telegenically killed"—a line that Israeli Prime Minister Benjamin Netanyahu himself then picked up to blame Hamas for producing "telegenic dead." Netanyahu and Krauthammer admit that Israel's victims are telegenic—young children tend to be—but they rely on an a priori dehumanization of Palestinians, a soul blindness so inflexible that even scenes of the massacred babies can be consumed without risk to the Zionist imaginary.

Soul blindness is hardly unique to slavers and contemporary ethno-supremacists; soul blindness is the perceptual schema of, among other things, global racial empire. Black and brown people are constantly forced into positions of proving their intentions and internal states in the face of entrenched, structural soul blindness, which is typically glossed as neutral doubt; it's a perverse "sort of 'enlarged' solipsism," as philosopher Rupert Read put it, in which uncertainty about the existence other minds is not a universal philosophical problem but hewed to colonial and racialized hierarchies.

Consider how Black patients in Western healthcare systems are significantly less likely to receive adequate pain treatment compared to other patients, especially for conditions where physicians are diagnosing the patient based primarily on pain behavior. Black women in particular are forced to (impossibly) *prove* that their pain is real in the face of systematic dismissal in medical settings. I say "impossibly" because if you're not taken seriously when expressing pain, there's really nothing more you can do to prove it. Except get sicker.

"Just try—in a real case—to doubt someone else's fear or pain," Wittgenstein writes. An odd remark indeed. Surely Wittgenstein, writing amid the rise of twentieth-century fascism, had seen people doubt the real pain and fear of others? The philosopher Read takes Wittgenstein's line to be a "genuine instruction or admonition . . . a measuredly emotional reminder, carrying with it a pathos, a reality check." Wittgenstein explicitly notes the possibility of malingering, but, as Read notes, "the possibility of [pain] simulation only brings out all the more clearly the need to acknowledge and care for the genuine article."

We do not, for the most part, walk around responding to expressions of pain and fear with doubt. Such skepticism is indeed hard to muster, as it should be, in the face of people in agony. Furthermore, we would not survive long as a species were such doubt the standard response to cries of pain. And more to the point, pain is not the sort of thing that it makes sense to ask for proof about—in cases without visible injury, what could such proof even look like? All we have is more pain behavior and language.

There is, as Wittgenstein famously pointed out, no private, mental "inner object" that we point to when we express that we're in pain. We do not learn to appreciate the meaning of the concept of pain because we somehow hold up our own little inner pain objects, compare them to other people's little inner pain objects and see that they are similar. Our pain language—our groans, sighs, descriptions—are part of collective language, the meaning of the word "pain." "You learned the concept 'pain' when you learned language," Wittgenstein writes. So, to deny or distrust a whole group of people when they express pain is quite literally to exclude them from collective sense making, from the very processes by which we make sense of suffering.

An obvious response to my charges of soul blindness here is that the left is just as guilty of it. When we frame our enemies as simply "oppressors," "colonizers," "capitalists" and so on, do we not also refuse to see the humans in these categories as fully human and ensouled? In an important sense, we do: we see such structural positions as indeed placing the people in those roles in a different ethical and political order, in a soulless condition. Psychiatrist and theorist Frantz Fanon famously highlighted how colonialism corrodes the minds of both colonist and colonized. That does not, however, leave us in some generalized and universal state of soul blindness, in which the oppressed are no less guilty of maintaining dehumanizing perceptual schema. Fanon observed that the overcoming of this wholly corrosive psychic state required the colonist's world be overthrown, the violence of colonial domination turned against its perpetrators. It is not, after all, because oppressed peoples fail to see their oppressors as fully human that oppressive structures continue. There are crucial structural asymmetries when it comes to epistemic standing in these cases; material realities of oppression produce and reproduce differentiated capacities to see-as and to know about the world.

This sort of soul blindness, ordered around race, performs and reflects what late philosopher Charles Mills called "white ignorance." White ignorance does not refer to "things people with white skin don't know" but rather "a cognitive tendency—an inclination, a doxastic disposition" historically and structurally engendered through European colonialism and racist domination. White ignorance is no less than an epistemic block, foreclosing knowledge of the brutal material realities of racial capitalism and negating the humanity and lived experience of Black people and other people of color.

Not all bearers of white ignorance are white, and not all cases of racist soul blindness look the same. My aim here is to interrogate potent cases that clarify the limits of witnessing and evidence-sharing in the face of white ignorance, which functions as a form of certainty. If we read Mill's idea of white ignorance alongside Wittgenstein's idea of certainty, we can see the contours of a framework of white certainty—or colonial certainty—within a social epistemology of ignorance. The cognitive tendency of white ignorance works like certainty in that it is borne of lived practices; its propositions do not have further justification, and it resists doubt. What we are talking about here is the "delusion of racial superiority [that] insulates itself against refutation," which is forged through histories of colonial domination, and has been maintained in the racial capitalist order. This is also precisely how Zionism functions as a moral certainty in Wittgenstein's sense: immune to recalcitrant evidence. I invoke Wittgenstein's question again: "Could there be human beings lacking in the capacity to see something as something?"

The plagues of soul blindness and white ignorance are not contained to only a small portion of specific, hateful individuals. I dare say we have all failed at times to live in the acknowledgement of the full humanity of others, at least to some extent; any beneficiaries of a capitalist order participate in a system of soul-blind exploitation.

Racist social epistemologies are made possible, Mills suggests, through the management of memory—a disavowal of the extraordinary extent to which colonialism ordered the world into racial regimes. As should no longer need pointing out, our establishment institutions—halls of power, courts, scientific and educational institutions—have consistently prioritized testimonies and histories that ideologically ground European colonial domination. "At one point in German South-West Africa," Mills notes, "white settlers demanded 'that in court only the testimony of seven African witnesses could outweigh evidence presented by a single white person' . . . Similarly, slave narratives often had to have white authenticators—for example, white abolitionists, with the racially based epistemic authority to write a preface or appear on stage with the author."

White ignorance is the systematic, habitually ingrained social amnesia that means racism today gets pathologized as hatred or bigotry, but—as Olúfẹ́mi O. Táíwò has argued—the layers and layers of sedimented, accumulated advantages and disadvantages along racial lines in colonialism's wakes are taken for granted.

(Mills points out that "male ignorance could be analyzed similarly" and we could say the same, as I address elsewhere, for "cis ignorance.")

Medical racism doesn't continue, for example, because medical students still read texts that assert that Black people have higher pain thresholds or other debunked posits of racist pseudoscience. Practices and habits of white ignorance are taken up, rather than explicitly learned. And these practices entrench and determine distrusting patient and doctor dynamics in turn.

Along the lines of Mills's notion of white ignorance, cultural theorist Nicholas Mirzoeff uses the concept of "white sight" to highlight concretely how we're not talking about a lack of seeing here, but an active way of seeing, materially forged and upheld, "layered and sedimented"—an "operating system of what it is to make whiteness and white supremacy." White sight, he notes, finds articulation in a vast array of visual culture, material infrastructures, and technologies, from the monuments to colonialists and Confederates that occupy key points in cities and towns to racist drawings depicting the imagined hierarchies of human physiognomy in so-called natural history texts of the nineteenth century to the deadly vision of the military drone's-eye view or the cops' bodycams today, and much more. As he told me, "It was often said that 'whiteness is unmarked.' And that's clearly not true. The whole point about whiteness is that it's absolutely marked, while creating a structure of unknowing among white people."

Mirzoeff's concept complements those of Mills and Cavell; he reminds us, at the very least, that there are infrastructures of white sight at which we must strike, that the frame of white sight needs to be destroyed, not served more content. Consider monuments to Confederates, colonizers, and slavers—an obvious but important example. They are part of the architecture of white sight, positing white men's dominance as the background of daily life. It is for good reason that Black liberation movements have taken aim at these monuments in the US, the UK, formerly colonized Africa, and elsewhere, for decades. Such acts are a strike against a world-picture that holds white supremacy tacitly certain.

As Mirzoeff notes, Fanon called colonial regimes a "world of statues." Per Fanon, "The statue of the general who carried out the conquest, the statue of the engineer who built the bridge; a world which is sure of itself, which crushes with its stones the backs flayed by whips: this is the colonial world." A world which is sure of itself—it does not make a case for itself, it does not argue for its rightness but is held in place with the technologies and material infrastructure of white sight. To repeat Wittgenstein's observation: "What stands fast does so not because it is intrinsically obvious or convincing; it is rather held fast by what lies around it."

When we watched protesters pull down Confederate monuments in 2020, we saw this world of statues brought rightfully into doubt. Towering statues in town squares, presented without context, do not, after all, offer insight into history but freeze historical norms in place, the management of memory grounding white ignorance. Left to stand undisturbed, monuments to Confederate generals and colonizers do not invite activities of knowledge production, like questioning and interrogation. Instead they, like the language games Wittgenstein describes, get to simply be "there, like our life." It is only when their standing is brought into doubt that fruitful activities of knowledge become possible.

Confederate statues themselves were acts of historical revisionism, mostly constructed decades after the end of the Civil War, either during post-Reconstruction Jim Crow or in a second wave of Confederate statue construction that served as a backlash to civil rights gains in the 1950s and 1960s. Nearly 20 percent of the 2,300 original Confederate memorials in the US were erected on courthouse lawns, the majority of these between the years 1900 and 1920—the height of Jim Crow. Counties with the highest number of Confederate memorials are also the ones that had the most instances of lynchings.

At the same time, actual historical records of the work of Black leaders in the Reconstruction era were regularly destroyed. Du Bois's description of the post-Reconstruction "propaganda of history" against Black people since emancipation serves as an apt description of today's work of white backlash: "one of the most stupendous efforts the world ever saw to discredit human beings, an effort involving universities, history, science, social life and religion."

The management of memory involves both erasure and construction to produce a terrain of racist certainty; such certainty is passed down through generations, not as a set of empirical facts to learn and *know* but as "an inherited background" to take for granted. There is a long and unbroken history of attempts to offer defenses and justifications of racial hierarchies using bogus science, but children, for example, do not take up racist behaviors and attitudes by being taught from Charles Murray's *The Bell Curve*.

Zionism's adherents may offer justifications for it, too, based on the long history of antisemitic oppression. These only look like justifications, though. Because when such justifications are challenged—when it is pointed out that they fail to justify the existence of a Jewish supremacist ethnostate and the Nakba on which it relies—Israel's right to exist is simply reasserted as unassailable. The activities of Zionist ideology involve no room for doubt (no room for the activities learning, doubting and scrutinizing of justifications at all); the necessity of the ethnostate is held as an irrefutable given, through an array of inculcating practices, coercions and training.

This leaves no room for knowledge, either. Or is this just another way of saying that ideologies are stubborn? Perhaps. But when we talk of "unlearning" ideology, Wittgenstein's framing of certainty reminds us that ideological certainties are not learned in the first place, not in the typical sense of the word. Racist soul blindness can and does flourish in communities where the entirety of propositional content taught appears to condemn racism ("all men are created equal," etc.), but white sight remains unbroken. Or, to borrow from Wittgenstein, "The game can be learned purely practically, without learning any explicit rules."

The question then becomes not how to simply add knowledge and correct ignorance, but how to disrupt the oppressive forms of life that produce racist epistemologies. Mills is clear that combatting epistemologies of ignorance requires structural, socio-economic shifts. You can't just add a few antiracist how-to books and diversity training sessions to dismantle an oppressive certainty. White ignorance and its ilk must not be treated with kid gloves.

"MAY SOMEONE have telling grounds for believing that the earth has only existed for a short time, say since his own birth?" Wittgenstein asks, scratching at another one of philosopher G. E. Moore's propositions. (Moore claimed to know for certain that, among other truisms, "the earth had existed also for many years before my body was born"; Wittgenstein points out that this is the sort of thing of which one is indeed certain and cannot doubt, but not by virtue of the activities of *knowing* it as a justified true belief.) But, Wittgenstein imagines, what about someone who wholeheartedly believes that the earth came into being at the moment of their birth: "Suppose he had always been told that,—would he have any good reason to doubt it? Men have believed that they could make the rain; why should not a king be brought up in the belief that the world began with him?"

It would take an extraordinarily sheltered life for such a king, yes, and still an immense amount of effort and training for those around the king, to uphold a world-picture in which the history of the world began with the king's birth. But Wittgenstein's point is that such a king, raised in such a way, would arguably be as certain about his picture of the world as we are certain that the earth existed long before we were born. The king's whole understanding of the world, as he experiences it, has hinged on this strange belief, constantly affirmed by courtiers and loyal subjects. Neither belief is arrived at by testing hypotheses about the earth's history. Yes, geologists and physicists do investigate the long history of the planet, but most of us laypeople are not certain that the earth existed long before our births because of geological investigations—rather, it is a certainty, taken for granted when we talk about past events at all (even, say, stories about how our parents met), that the earth has long preexisted us. This weird king grows up, meanwhile, with very different stories.

"And if Moore and this king were to meet and discuss, could Moore really prove his belief to be the right one?" Wittgenstein continues. "I do not say that Moore could not convert the king to his view, but it would be a conversion of a special kind; the king would be brought to look at the world in a different way."

What does this mean? It means the king, ensconced in his rarefied world, will not be convinced by Moore presenting him with empirical facts, such as descriptions of events dating from before his birth. The king was raised to brush these off and incorporate them into his young-earth mythology. It would require removing him from his sheltered palaces and introducing him into a world where his proclamations about historic time are not taken as sense making but senseless. This is a world in which meaning is not oriented around the king, such that it becomes increasingly impossible to fit all the experiences he has and all the testimonies he hears into his picture of a merely decades-old world; the world he experiences crashes against his world-picture. In a form of life not built for the king, he would not last long trying to function and communicate about the world while relying on the assumption that the earth came into being with his birth. Crucially though, it is his form of life that has to shift for such a new understanding to gain traction.

The mistake for self-identifying allies is to imagine the work needed is to prove to the racist (or system of white ignorance) the existence of nonwhite people's interiority and humanity, particularly by displaying their suffering. The fault here is twofold, as Samudzi's intervention makes clear: Firstly, centuries of such displays have failed to disrupt oppression. Secondly, such an approach aims at serving (curing?) the soul-blind and using the suffering of oppressed peoples as the treatment to do so; it prioritizes an internal relation with the racists rather than their victims. And this was Samudzi's point: it's not just the Derek Chauvins and the Charlie Kirks who are soul-blind in this scenario; it is the well-meaning white witnesses treating Black suffering as the stuff of evidence to circulate—as if they were playing good cop.

These acts of antiracist witnessing work to circulate knowledge about a circumstance without necessarily involving what Cavell called "acknowledgement," by which he meant a form of interventionary action. I can know something and not act on it; to acknowledge something requires, even in the most minimal sense, an *act* of acknowledgement. As Cavell puts it, "It is not enough that I know (am certain) that you suffer—I must do or reveal something (whatever can be done)":

> A "failure to know" might just mean a piece of ignorance, an absence of something, a blank. A "failure to acknowledge" is the presence of something, a confusion, an indifference, a callousness, an exhaustion, a coldness.

Acknowledgement, as we tend to use the term, is hardly a sufficient response to our racist necropolitical order. It's reading an Indigenous land acknowledgement at the start of a corporate shareholder meeting—the ultimate "action without disruption" that Samudzi rightly decries. But successful acknowledgement, in the sense Cavell means, would indeed require more than just a repetition of statements and facts. True acknowledgement requires action. The rebels who tear down Confederate monuments make what is already visible and dominant in the world-picture of white sight newly visible *for what it is*, an infrastructure in need of dismantling; that is acknowledgement. The students around the world who risked their academic careers by ensuring that university life would not continue as normal while funds flowed to Israel's war machine—they were acknowledging their internal relation to Palestinians in struggle. This is not just making visible the plight of Palestinians through acts of protest; the acknowledgement lies rather in refusing a form of life in which complicity in the Zionist project is held certain.

A certainty seemingly immune from doubt can be destabilized. The many thousands of anti-Zionist Jewish people like myself who have "unlearned" the Zionism with which they were raised and now fight for Palestinian liberation are evidence of this. And yes, for the most part this happened through a process of exposure to the truths of Israel's violence and the oppression of Palestinians. But under what conditions does exposure work? There's no foolproof method, but, anecdotally at least, the turn from Zionism does not happen in isolation, with a lone thinker sifting through examples of brutality. As with Wittgenstein's solipsistic imaginary king, a different kind of conversion is necessary.

"The sickness of a time is cured by an alteration in the mode of life of human beings," Wittgenstein wrote in his *Remarks on the Foundation of Mathematics*, "and it was possible for the sickness of philosophical problems to get cured only through a changed mode of thought and of life, not through a medicine invented by an individual." Most anti-Zionists don't leave Zionist worldviews without listening to or reading Palestinians speak of their struggle—that is, it requires a form of life, engaging in activity, which treats Palestinians as agents, as people, as partners and leaders in collective struggle.

Echoing James Baldwin's grim recognition that his survival has been dependent on outwitting white people, Mills notes that "correspondingly, on the positive epistemic side, the route to black knowledge is the self-conscious recognition of white ignorance." To see white ignorance as the blind spot that it is, and to use the epistemic block against itself.

Political theorist Geo Maher has written recently on "racial hubris" and the "cunning of resistance"—anticolonial struggle and successful slave revolts relied on the " 'zero-point hubris' characteristic of colonial thought," this cultivated blindness, which the oppressed could see clearly and take advantage of. I recently watched a video from 1976, shot in what was then Rhodesia under white minority rule. Then prime minister Sir Ian Smith said that year that "there will never be Black majority rule in this country in over a thousand of years." The other whites interviewed in the footage see no end to their ruling status in sight. Just two years later, Smith was forced, in response to the war of liberation, to concede to majority rule; independent Zimbabwe was established in 1980.

"Decolonial cunning," writes Maher, "takes full advantage of the blindspot of its purveyors"—the blind spots of white sight—"wrapping itself in the cloak of invisibility that white supremacy has imposed and cultivating resistance in those same clandestine shadows." The infrastructures and technologies of white sight—border walls, drone's-eye views, totalizing surveillance—are fixed in their aspect perception; they do not allow for the dawning of a new aspect. There is much to be said for rejecting struggle on such rigged terms of visibility and recalling instead, as Maher reminds us, Marx's "old mole, who knows so well how to work underground." From Vietnam to Palestine, the importance of (literal) underground resistance taking advantage of colonial blind spots cannot be underestimated. "What if we de-center the white anxieties that animate the walling campaigns of the present, to instead re-center the ontological and literal underground?" asks Maher.

Wittgenstein doesn't offer suggestions as to the "conversion of a special kind" that would be needed to bring his imagined king to hold the same certainties as we do, to share in our world-picture. He writes only that the king "would be brought to look at the world in a different way." What if we decenter the king? His conversion could happen anyway, in such a hypothetical world, were the monarchy to be overthrown. He may be forced to see differently, to see a different world, because his world has been forever changed. And so it is with the soul-blind: The point is not to beg for acknowledgement from those who are incapable of offering it, but rather to expand and strengthen our spheres of mutual acknowledgement—call it solidarity. This might not bring soul sight to the soul-blind, but that's not the primary concern. The point is to make those who are unacknowledged in a soul-blind system a greater force to reckon with.

Conclusion: Not Starting from Scratch

A number of Marxist theorists have decried Wittgenstein's work as the antithesis of Marx's injunction that "philosophers have only interpreted the world, in various ways. The point, however, is to change it." Wittgenstein, after all, said that "philosophy leaves everything as it is."

"The whole Wittgensteinian theory of language," writes Perry Anderson, "presupposes an unchanging corpus of concepts and an unalterable pattern of the contexts governing them." Philosophy like Wittgenstein's, he writes, "functions as an anaesthetic ideology, blotting out the very memory of an alternative order of thought."

It's a fierce condemnation. But an unfair one, I would say. Not because Wittgenstein himself was committed to liberatory political change; he wasn't. His work does, however, make explicit the fact that concepts *do* change, *specifically* altered by the contexts governing them. "When language-games change, then there is a change in concepts, and with the concepts the meanings of words change," he notes. As a constitutive part of material history, our language games—which are not distinct from our forms of life—give rise to new and changeable conceptual possibilities.

Anderson is right, though, that Wittgenstein offers no framework for and no guidance on how to make changes for the collective better; he offers no critique of power, no master key to ending racial capitalism and fascist domination. This is because philosophy could not, as he saw it, step outside itself and do anything of the sort. Acts of philosophy, like acts of journalism, might be necessary in clarifying terrains of struggle and the operations of power, but they are insufficient for shifting those grounds. What this work can do, though, is demystify and help us look seriously at what the hell we're doing, saying, assuming and taking for granted. In what claims our beliefs and practices are grounded, and when we are proceeding without further grounds or justifications.

That Wittgenstein himself was no fan of political organizing need not be of any real relevance to us, beyond the fact that we will not list him among our revolutionary inspirations. We must find our guides elsewhere. In Wittgenstein's philosophy I nonetheless see a clear refrain: it is in our activities and our practices that we maintain what is or is not held certain, and it is also by such practices that what is certain can shift, and with that shift, what is possible.

But, yes, the big question remains, which is really a multitude of questions across contexts: How is it to be done? "Through practices" is hardly a sufficient response here. As the philosopher von Redecker puts it, with reference to Wittgenstein's framework of certainty: "But where should new experiences and alternative practices come from, if the course of things is determined by the riverbed"—the riverbed of structures that are firmly anchored? And how can these activities and practices offer more than just fleeting, interstitial breaks, swiftly repressed and swept away? How can we replace existing stabilized practices and habits, ordered as they are by coercive capitalist property relations and state violence? Which activities, which practices should we be continuing or taking up?

Von Redecker notes that it is only in the practices, rehearsed in periods of apparent rupture, or "interstices," that we can recognize how to go on, and go on again. Calling on Thomas Kuhn's notion of paradigm shifts in science, von Redecker reminds us, "Even in science as described by Kuhn, the solutions are usually already there for a long time, but they elude perception as solutions." According to Kuhn, scientific revolutions involve what were previously taken, under a previous paradigm, as troublesome anomalies being taken up and rearranged as structuring, as it were, certainties in a new paradigm.

There is no assurance, even in science, of revolutionary progress; paradigms remain and are stubbornly upheld even in the face of anomalies that many might see as a crisis. And so it is for political revolution. As von Redecker puts it, "Revolutions are long processes. Even intense moments of culmination gain their effectiveness from practices that are laboriously rehearsed over time, and from the coming together of structures that are anchored in specific ways." But again, nothing is assured; radical and lasting social shifts "depend on the precarious course taken by practices, as they are reproduced and transferred." The point, though, is that when we talk of taking up and repeating and sharing practices here, that means "recognizing that we are not at the beginning."

On the night Trump was reelected president, my old friend since the days of Occupy Wall Street, the writer and editor Sarah Leonard, reminded me, with a hug, "We are not starting from scratch."

We do not need to reach far back in time for inspiration. In the US alone, in the last decade, consider the extraordinary mutual aid efforts that kept vulnerable neighbors fed at the height of the Covid pandemic; or the tenants movements growing nationwide; the workers—from nurses, to teachers, to cab drivers, to dockworkers—who have reinvigorated collective and militant labor actions; or the networks circulating abortion pills and hormones to those who need them. I recall the 2020 Black liberation uprisings, the water protectors at Standing Rock, and the resistance in Atlanta and beyond to the construction of Cop City. I think, too, of the Gaza solidarity actions, millions strong. I point to the powerful example set by the people of Minneapolis when their city was besieged by Trump's deportation machine in early 2026. Relying on networks of solidarity and practices of resistance developed in part during the George Floyd revolt, Minnesotans organized a statewide one-day mass strike—the largest in a century—in a matter of days. No, the government was not brought to its knees under the economic weight of a one-day strike called on short notice; nationwide general strikes did not immediately follow. It did, however, exemplify the sort of political strike that takes aim at the specific nature of fascist state operations in our cities and towns. It is precisely this combined model of strike, targeted blockade, and mass demonstration, all undergirded by networks of mutual aid, that we need to repeat and expand. Such practices were not only learned to fight Trump's regime. They have been rehearsed many times over, in centuries of struggle.

General strikes today, in an age of technocapital and decimated labor power, will not look the same as they did in the early twentieth century. Even with a slowly rebuilding labor movement, effectively marshaling collective refusal is extremely hard. A general strike against contemporary authoritarianism requires a specific navigation of territory and time—addressing, for example, the ways government forces move rapidly through neighborhoods and weaponize existing infrastructures. Not every day can take the form of a general strike, but that is our horizon. "The general strike is the name for when the riot, the strike, and the commune all happen at once," the late theorist Joshua Clover said in a 2024 interview. Community care, militant disruption, working-class refusal. "That's what the general strike really is. And that's the day, the week, or the year where there will be a role for everyone." There is a role for everyone, because that time must be now.

"Optimism of the will," I have heard comrades answer when asked how they approach these so-called uncertain times—and I have said the same. Yes, it is clichéd, and perhaps a cop-out, to throw out a well-used Gramsci quote in this way. Gramsci wrote in a 1929 letter to his younger brother, "My mind is pessimistic, but my will is optimistic. Whatever the situation, I imagine the worst that could happen in order to summon up all my reserves and will power to overcome every obstacle." And he wrote this in a fascist prison—already, for many of us, the very meaning of "the worst that could happen."

If I am honest, I do not have such faith in my nerves and willpower. But we keep organizing and meeting and talking and planning and writing and teaching and boycotting and blockading and striking and refusing—as we do refuse—to abandon the more liberatory forms of our lives. Such practices are optimistic simply insofar as we have not stopped doing them. This is what abolitionist writer Mariame Kaba means in popularizing the phrase "Hope is a discipline": the feeling of hope is irrelevant; what matters are the practices of going on.

Knowing *how* to go on does not require knowing *that* we will succeed. "If militant tactics are legitimate only on the precondition of certainty about their efficacy, they would have to be excluded in most if not all cases," writes Andreas Malm in an essay defending acts of property destruction and sabotage. "Rare is the resistance launched in perfect knowledge of victory. In fact, much resistance in the past and present has been undertaken against overwhelming odds, with nothing resembling a guarantee of success. Just consider, again, the Palestinian resistance, in all its multifarious forms." This most crucial struggle would have died long ago if participation were predicated on the surety, or if even the moderate probability, of success. Malm continues, "Nor, I would wager, did the enslaved people in Haiti gathering at Bois Caïman on the night of 14 August 1791 know for a fact that they would win—how could they possibly? Thankfully, they rose up despite the uncertainty that pervades every moment of rebellion."

The grassroots interventions of recent years may seem cold comfort—repressed and short-lived as they have often been, while authoritarian capitalism continues to reign. But we have also witnessed a shift away from the presumptions of liberal centrism in ways that may have seemed impossible just a few years ago. What was for many a certainty, a riverbed through which political possibilities were channeled, has been eroded.

I think, too, about New Yorkers organizing en masse to elect a democratic socialist mayor in the face of a powerful, billionaire-funded campaign peddling Islamophobic lies. One need not put great faith in electoral politics to recognize the meaning of such a breakthrough achieved with practices of building power, which we must pick up and continue.

In the popular and necessarily open-ended words of revolutionary poet Diane di Prima, "NO ONE WAY WORKS, it will take all of us/ shoving at the thing from all sides/ to bring it down." I'm not saying we know how to win. I'm saying we know how to go on—we are not starting from scratch.

Recall again Wittgenstein's reflections on what we talk about when we talk about the nature of "understanding" something—the ability to understand a concept, a rule, a formula:

> Ask yourself: in what sort of case, in what kind of circumstances, do we say, "Now I know how to go on"?

He continues:

> "Now I know how to go on!" is an exclamation; it corresponds to an instinctive sound, a glad start. Of course it does not follow from my feeling that I shall not find I am stuck when I do try to go on.—Here there are cases in which I should say: "When I said I knew how to go on, I did know." One will say that if, for example, an unforeseen interruption occurs. But what is unforeseen must not simply be that I get stuck.

We can, many of us, recall circumstances in which we did know how to go on in antifascist, liberatory practices. We can recognize them; we can go on with them. We have cared for each other, refused complicity, refused to work, worked, taken risks, taught, shared, marched, blockaded, found each other and acted in great numbers. Again and again, though, acting against anchored practices of hegemony, we have faced ferocious interruptions. These will go on, too.

There have also been times when we have simply been stuck. We have lacked understanding. But it is not overwhelming uncertainty, faced with the complexities of the world from a god's-eye view, that has tripped us up. To look ahead to an abstracted future of totalizing uncertainty is to commit to an abstraction—it makes little sense. It is, to borrow another Wittgensteinian metaphor, like trying to walk on "slippery ice where there is no friction . . . because of that, we are unable to walk. We want to walk: so we need friction. Back to the rough ground!" The rough ground of the everyday, as certain as it is uncertain. There, on some of the harshest of terrains, we have been shown what it is to go on.

Acknowledgments

To all my comrades who have thought with me through the doubts and the certainties of recent years; on the page, in the streets and encampments, within struggles, across dinner tables and bars, and at our beloved, imperiled New School for Social Research. Thank you to my marvelous Verso editor, Leo Hollis, and wonderful previous editor, John Merrick, for their wisdom and support. I'd also like to thank, in no particular order, a (no doubt incomplete) list of those generous and brilliant friends who read or discussed this work with me at length: Sophia Larigakis, Sophie Lewis, Carmel Lobello, Hannah Cohen, Adam Tooze, Katrina Forrester, Andreas Petrossiants, Molly Crabapple, Ali Gharib, May Jeong, Evangeline Riddiford-Graham, Alice Crary, Ricarda Messner, Pandora Lennard, and with an extra pouring of gratitude for Jim Miller.

I echo Ludwig Wittgenstein's sentiment in the 1945 preface to his *Philosophical Investigations*: "For more than one reason what I publish here will have points of contact with what other people are writing to-day.—If my remarks do not bear a stamp which marks them as mine,—I do not wish to lay any further claim to them as my property. I make them public with doubtful feelings."

For Lukas Hermsmeier, my bedrock and my river, my axis and my orbit, my knowing and my certainty.

Works Cited

Introduction: On Un/Certainty

Crary, Alice, and Rupert Read, *The New Wittgenstein*, Routledge, 2000.

Fisher, Mark, *Capitalist Realism: Is There No Alternative?* (revised), Zero Books, 2022.

Heyes, Cressida, *The Grammar of Politics: Wittgenstein and Political Philosophy*, Cornell University Press, 2003.

Read, Rupert, *Wittgenstein's Liberatory Philosophy: Thinking Through His Philosophical Investigations*, Routledge, 2020.

Srinivasan, Amia, "Genealogy, Epistemology and Worldmaking," *Proceedings of the Aristotelian Society* 119, no. 2, 2019.

Táíwò, Olúfẹ́mi O., *Reconsidering Reparations*, Oxford University Press, 2022.

Velocci, Beans, "The Uncertain Times," *Avidly*, 2020.

Wittgenstein, Ludwig, *Philosophical Investigations*, trans. G. E. M. Anscombe, P. M. S. Hacker, Joachim Schulte, Wiley-Blackwell, 2009.

Wittgenstein, Ludwig, *On Certainty*, in *Major Works: Selected Philosophical Writings*, Harper Perennial, 2009.

1. Certain Crises

Adler-Bolton, Beatrice, and Artie Vierkant, *Health Communism*, Verso Books, 2022.

Adler-Bolton, Beatrice, and Artie Vierkant, "The Year the Pandemic 'Ended,' " *The New Inquiry*, 2022.

Berlant, Lauren, "Slow Death (Sovereignty, Obesity, Lateral Agency)," *Critical Inquiry* 33, no. 4, 2007.

Berlant, Lauren, *Cruel Optimism*, Duke University Press, 2011.

Blix, Hagen, and Ingeborg Glimmer, *Why We Fear AI: On the Interpretation of Nightmares, Commons Notions,* 2015.

Cohen, Rachel, "The Year Our Reality Broke," *New York Times*, 2021.

Cooper, Melinda, *Counterrevolution: Extravagance and Austerity in Public Finance*, Zone Books, 2024.

Crary, Alice, "If You're Not Outraged About AI, You're Not Paying Attention," Annual Public Lecture, Royal Institute of Philosophy, School of Philosophy, University College Dublin, Ireland, 2025.

Cutler, David, and Ed Glaeser, "Cutting the NIH—The $8 Trillion Health Care Catastrophe," *JAMA Health Forum*, 2025.

Derrida, Jacques, *Negotiations: Interventions and Interviews 1971–2001*, trans. Elizabeth Rottenberg, Stanford University Press, 2002.

Dewey, John, ed. Melvin L. Rogers, *The Public and Its Problems: An Essay in Political Inquiry*, Penn State University Press, 2012.

Eich, Stefan, "Expedience and Experimentation: John Maynard Keynes and the Politics of Time," *American Journal of Political Science* 69, no. 1, 2025.

Fassin, Didier, and Axel Honneth, eds., *Crisis Under Critique: How People Assess, Transform, and Respond to Critical Situations*, Columbia University Press, 2022.

Guha, Ranajit, *Dominance without Hegemony: History and Power in Colonial India*, Harvard University Press, 1998.

Hall, Stuart, and Gregory McLennan, *Stuart Hall: Selected Writings on Marxism*, Duke University Press, 2021.

Hont, Istvan, "The Permanent Crisis of a Divided Mankind: 'Contemporary Crisis of the Nation State' in Historical Perspective," *Political Studies* 42, 1994.

Jameson, Fredric, "The Aesthetics of Singularity," *New Left Review* 92, 2015.

Koselleck, Reinhart, "Crisis," trans. Michaela Richter, *Journal of the History of Ideas* 67, no. 2, 2006.

Koselleck, Reinhart, *Critique and Crisis: Enlightenment and the Pathogenesis of Modern Society*, trans. Thomas McCarthy, MIT Press, 2000.

Mann, Geoff, "Irrational Expectations," *Viewpoint*, 2020.

Mann, Geoff, "Climate of Uncertainty," Lecture, University of Victoria, 2024.

Roitman, Janet, *Anti-Crisis*, Duke University Press, 2013.

Roitman, Janet, "Crisis," *Political Concepts: A Critical Lexicon*, 2012.

Rouse, Carolyn, "Necropolitics versus Biopolitics: Spatialization, White Privilege, and Visibility during a Pandemic," *Cultural Anthropology* 36, no. 3, 2021.

Roy, Arundhati, "The Pandemic Is a Portal," *Financial Times*, 2020.

Táíwò, Olúfẹ́mi O., *Reconsidering Reparations*, Oxford University Press, 2022.

Taylor, Astra, *The Age of Insecurity: Coming Together As Things Fall Apart*, House of Anansi Press, 2023.

Tooze, Adam, "Welcome to the Age of Polycrisis," *Financial Times*, 2022.

Tooze, Adam, *Shutdown: How Covid Shook the World's Economy*, Viking, 2021.

Tooze, Adam, "Chartbook on Shutdown: Keynes and Why We Can Afford Anything We Can Do," *Chartbook*, 2021.

Tooze, Adam, "Chartbook 400: Murder Not Crisis—Why Israel's Starvation of Gaza Is Exceptional in a Global Context," *Chartbook*, 2025.

Tooze, Adam, "Chartbook 407: Polycrisis Revisited: Are We beyond Neoliberal Order Breakdown Syndrome?," *Chartbook*, 2025.

von Redecker, Eva, *Praxis and Revolution: A Theory of Social Transformation*, trans. Lucy Duggan, Columbia University Press, 2021.

Wittgenstein, Ludwig, *Philosophical Investigations*, trans. G. E. M. Anscombe, P. M. S. Hacker, Joachim Schulte, Wiley-Blackwell, 2009.

Wittgenstein, Ludwig, *On Certainty* in *Major Works: Selected Philosophical Writings*, Harper Perennial, 2009.

2. Border Certainties

Arthur, Andrew R., "*The Wall Street Journal*'s Evolving Views on 'Open Borders'," Center for Immigration Studies, 2022.

Bhandar, Brenna, *Colonial Lives of Property: Law, Land, and Racial Regimes of Ownership*, Duke University Press, 2018.

Bier, David J., "Deportations to Add Almost $1 Trillion in Costs to the 'Big Beautiful Bill'," CATO Institute, 2025.

Brown, Wendy, *Undoing the Demos: Neoliberalism's Stealth Revolution*, Zone Books, 2015.

Du Bois, W. E. B., *Darkwater: Voices from Within the Veil*, Verso Books, 2016.

Goldstein, Alyosha, "By Force of Expectation: Colonization, Public Lands, and the Property Relation," Discourse, *UCLA Law Review*, 2018.

Harris, Cheryl I., "Whiteness as Property," *Harvard Law Review* 106, no. 8, 1993.

Hont, Istvan, "The Permanent Crisis of a Divided Mankind: 'Contemporary Crisis of the Nation State' in Historical Perspective," *Political Studies* 42, 1994.

Loick, Daniel, *The Abuse of Property*, trans. Jacob Blumenfeld, MIT Press, 2023.

Mackey, Eva, *Unsettled Expectations: Uncertainty, Land and Settler Decolonization*, Fernwood Publishing, 2016.

Miller, Todd, *Empire of Borders: The Expansion of the US Border around the World*, Verso Books, 2019.

Österman, Marcus, "Myth Busted: EU Migrants No Extra Burden on Taxpayers in More Generous Welfare States," *Conversation*, 2019.

Osterweil, Vicky, *In Defense of Looting: A Riotous History of Uncivil Action*, Bold Type Books, 2020.

Roitman, Janet, *Anti-Crisis*, Duke University Press, 2013.

Singh, Akshi, "Unlived Security," *Parapraxis*, 2024.

Slobodian, Quinn, "Hayek's Bastards: The Populist Right's Neoliberal Roots," *Tribune*, 2021.

Taylor, Astra, *The Age of Insecurity: Coming Together as Things Fall Apart*, House of Anansi Press, 2023.

von Redecker, Eva, "Ownership's Shadow: Neoauthoritarianism as Defense of Phantom Possession," *Critical Times, Interventions in Global Critical Theory* 3, no. 1, 2020.

von Redecker, Eva, *Praxis and Revolution: A Theory of Social Transformation*, trans. Lucy Duggan, Columbia University Press, 2021.

Walia, Harsha, *Border and Rule: Global Migration, Capitalism, and the Rise of Racist Nationalism*, Haymarket Books, 2021.

Washington, John, *The Case for Open Borders*, Haymarket Books, 2024.

Wittgenstein, Ludwig, *On Certainty*, in *Major Works: Selected Philosophical Writings*, Harper Perennial, 2009.

Wittgenstein, Ludwig, *Philosophical Investigations*, trans. G. E. M. Anscombe, P. M. S. Hacker, Joachim Schulte, Wiley-Blackwell, 2009.

3. Cis Certainty, Trans Knowledge

Burke, Megan, "Cis Sense and the Habit of Gender Assignment," *The Journal of Speculative Philosophy* 36, no. 2, 2022.

Butler, Judith, *Gender Trouble*, Routledge Classics, 2006.

Du Bois, W. E. B., *The Souls of Black Folk*, ed. Hayes Edwards, Brent, Oxford University Press, 2008.

Edelman, Lee, *No Future: Queer Theory and the Death Drive*, Duke University Press, 2004.

Freeman, Hadley, "People have told me I'm on the wrong side of history, but I still want to be their friend," *Guardian*, 2021.

Fox, Max, "The Traffic in Children," *Parapraxis*, 2023.

Gamero Cabrera, Isabel G., "Acknowledging Women. Some Wittgensteinian Ideas to Clarify the Cis/Trans Debate," *Nordic Wittgenstein Review*, 2022.

Gill-Peterson, Jules, *Histories of the Transgender Child*, University of Minnesota Press, 2018.

Gill-Peterson, Jules, " 'Imagine What We'll Build for One Another," interview with Beatrice Adler-Bolton, *The New Inquiry*, 2022.

Gill-Peterson, Jules, "The Child," *Parapraxis*, 2023.

Heyes, Cressida, " 'Back to the Rough Ground!': Wittgenstein, Essentialism, and Feminist Methods," in *Feminist Interpretations of*

Ludwig Wittgenstein, ed. Peg O'Connor and Naomi Scheman, Penn State University Press, 2002.

Hipwell, Kim, "Why Gamete Production Does Not Define Sex," *Medium*, 2023.

Lavery, Grace, "Gender Criticism versus Gender Abolition: On Three Recent Books about Gender," *Los Angeles Review of Books*, 2023.

Lewis, Sophie, *Full Surrogacy Now: Feminism against Family*, Verso Books, 2019.

Lewis, Sophie, "There Can Be No Nonviolence in Human Gestation," interview with Natasha Lennard, Public Seminar, 2022.

Padawer, Ruth, "The Humiliating Practice of Sex-Testing Female Athletes," *New York Times Magazine*, 2016.

Stock, Kathleen, interview with Emma Burnett, *BBC Women's Hour*, 2021.

Lugones, Maria, "The Coloniality of Gender," in *The Palgrave Handbook of Gender and Development*, ed. Wendy Harcourt, Palgrave Macmillan, 2016.

Serano, Julia, "Why All the Anti-Trans Arguments Are Bogus," interview with *Current Affairs*, 2021.

Velocci, Beans, "Standards of Care: Uncertainty and Risk in Harry Benjamin's Transsexual Classifications," *Transgender Studies Quarterly* 8, no. 4, 2021.

Wittgenstein, Ludwig, *On Certainty* in *Major Works: Selected Philosophical Writings*, Harper Perennial, 2009.

Wittgenstein, Ludwig, *Philosophical Investigations*, trans. G. E. M. Anscombe, P. M. S. Hacker, Joachim Schulte, Wiley-Blackwell, 2009.

4. Seeing-As

Albanese, Francesca, and Irene Khan, "States Must Stop Israel before All Journalists in Gaza Are Silenced: UN Experts," United Nations Human Rights Office of the High Commissioner, 2025.

Cavell, Stanley, *The Claim of Reason: Wittgenstein, Skepticism, Morality, and Tragedy*, Oxford University Press, 1999.

Du Bois, W. E. B., *Black Reconstruction in America: An Essay Toward a History of the Part Which Black Folk Played in the Attempt to*

Reconstruct Democracy in America, 1860–1880, 1st edition, ed. Henry Louis Gates Jr, Oxford University Press, 2014.

Fanon, Frantz, *The Wretched of the Earth*, trans. Constance Farrington, Penguin Modern Classics, 2001.

Havercroft, Jonathan and David Owen, "Soul-Blindness, Police Orders and Black Lives Matter: Wittgenstein, Cavell, and Rancière," *Political Theory* 44, no. 6, 2016.

Krauthammer, Charles, "Moral Clarity in Gaza," *Washington Post*, 2014.

Lennard, Natasha, "Bari Weiss's Free Press Wants You to Know Some Kids Being Starved by Israel Were Already Sick," *Intercept*, 2025.

Lithwick, Dahlia, "Stop Playing Violent Videos of Black People's Deaths," *Slate*, 2021.

Maher, Geo, *Anticolonial Eruptions: Racial Hubris and the Cunning of Resistance*, University of California Press, 2022.

Mills, Charles W., *Black Rights/White Wrongs: The Critique of Racial Liberalism*, Oxford Academic, 2017.

Mirzoeff, Nicholas, *White Sight: Visual Politics and Practices of Whiteness*, MIT Press, 2023.

Mirzoeff, Nicholas, "The General Crisis of Whiteness: A Conversation with Nicholas Mirzoeff," interview with Natasha Lennard, *Los Angeles Review of Books*, 2023.

Read, Rupert, "Wittgenstein's 'Philosophical Investigations' as a War Book," *New Literary History* 41, no. 3, 2010.

Read, Rupert, *Wittgenstein's Liberatory Philosophy: Thinking through His Philosophical Investigations*, Routledge, 2020.

Samudzi, Zoé "White Witness and the Contemporary Lynching," *The New Republic*, 2020.

Scahill, Jeremy "Joe Biden Keeps Repeating False Claim He Saw Photos of Beheaded Babies," *The Intercept*, 2023.

Sidwha, Feroze, "65 Doctors, Nurses and Paramedics: What We Saw in Gaza," *New York Times*, 2024.

Táíwò, Olúfẹ́mi O., *Reconsidering Reparations*, Oxford University Press, 2022.

Turfah, Mary, "Complicity," *Parapraxis*, 2025.

United Nations Human Rights Council Independent International Commission of Inquiry on the occupied Palestinian territory, including East Jerusalem, and Israel, "Legal Analysis of the Conduct of Israel in Gaza Pursuant to the Convention on the Prevention and Punishment of the Crime of Genocide," 2025.

Wallace-Wells, Benjamin, "How a Conservative Activist Invented the Conflict Over Critical Race Theory," *New Yorker*, 2021.

Wittgenstein, Ludwig, *On Certainty*, in *Major Works: Selected Philosophical Writings*, Harper Perennial, 2009.

Wittgenstein, Ludwig, *Philosophical Investigations*, trans. G. E. M. Anscombe, P. M. S. Hacker, Joachim Schulte, Wiley-Blackwell, 2009.

Wittgenstein, Ludwig, *Remarks on the Foundations of Mathematics*, ed. G. H. von Wright, R. Rhees, and G. E. M. Anscombe, MIT Press, 1983.

Conclusion: Not Starting from Scratch

Anderson, Perry, "Components of the National Culture," *New Left Review* 50, 1968.

Clover, Joshua, " 'People Struggle Where They Are': Joshua Clover on Riots, Strikes and Communes That Are Already Here," interview with Ronja Mälström, *Turning Point*, 2024.

Di Prima, Diane, *Revolutionary Letters*, 50th anniversary edition, City Lights, 2021.

Kaba, Mariame, *We Do This 'Til We Free Us: Abolitionist Organizing and Transforming Justice*, ed. Tamara Nopper, Haymarket Books, 2021.

Malm, Andreas, "In Defense of Sabotage: A Response to George Monbiot," Verso Books Blog, 2023.

Olson, Gary, "Pessimism, Optimism and the Role of Intellectuals," *Counterpunch*, 2019.

von Redecker, Eva, *Praxis and Revolution: A Theory of Social Transformation*, trans. Lucy Duggan, Columbia University Press, 2021.

Wittgenstein, Ludwig, *On Certainty*, in *Major Works: Selected Philosophical Writings*, Harper Perennial, 2009.

Wittgenstein, Ludwig, *Philosophical Investigations*, trans. G. E. M. Anscombe, P. M. S. Hacker, Joachim Schulte, Wiley-Blackwell, 2009.

Index